THE LIFE
AND LETTERS OF
TOFU ROSHI

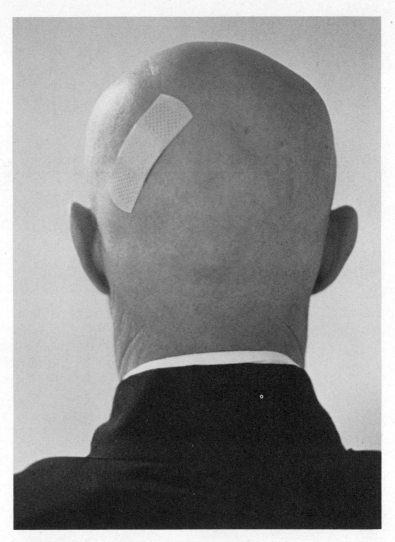

"*Why is there something rather than nothing?*"

THE LIFE
AND LETTERS OF
TOFU ROSHI

Susan Ichi Su Moon

FOREWORD BY GAHAN WILSON

Photographs by Marc Landau
With additional photographs by
Sandy de Lissovoy

SHAMBHALA
Boston & Shaftesbury
1988

SHAMBHALA PUBLICATIONS, INC.

Horticultural Hall
300 Massachusetts Avenue
Boston, Massachusetts 02115

The Old School House
The Courtyard, Bell Street
Shaftesbury, Dorset SP7 8BP

9 8 7 6 5 4 3 2 1

FIRST EDITION

Printed in the United States of America
Distributed in the United States by Random House
and in Canada by Random House of Canada Ltd.
Distributed in the United Kingdom by Element Books Ltd.

Library of Congress Cataloging-in-Publication Data
Moon, Susan Ichi Su, 1942–
    The life and letters of Tofu Roshi.
    1. Zen Buddhism—United States—Humor. I. Title.
PN6161.M655 1988   818'.5407   88-18224
ISBN 0-87773-461-5 (pbk.)

For my friends, past and present,
at the Berkeley Zen Center

AUTHOR'S NOTE

The No Way Zen Center and the people who inhabit it are purely fictitious. There is No Such Place and there are No Such People.

CONTENTS

FOREWORD

Many teachers, in their pride, vainly boast that they know nothing, but it is Tofu alone who has truly succeeded in achieving total ignorance. Furthermore, only Tofu has mastered the art of passing on his unsullied condition to those willing to receive it. One particularly gifted student achieved perfect stupidity when only halfway through his first bow of *gassho* to the Master and ever since responds to all questions ("Does one brand of soap contain more Buddha nature than another?," "Am I wearing my original face right side up or upside down?," "Will this bus take me to Forty-second Street?") with the same vaguely irritating blank look.

It is not merely that the Roshi's teaching is totally devoid of content or any hint of meaning—many other teachers have achieved that; its most remarkable aspect is the impossibility of remembering a single word he's spoken, or even if he spoke at all. Recordings do not seem to help since every tape of his *teishos* so far contain only background throat-clearings, or pillow shiftings, or the patient humming of air conditioners.

I know that I personally went through a two-week *sesshin* with the Roshi last summer because I have the check stubs to prove it, but I have no recollection whatsoever of the event, and, even more remarkable, *I am convinced that I spent the entire period with a girl named Sheila Galsworthy in Akron, Ohio.* I would like to see Western Science explain *that*.

The same phenomenon is observable in Tofu's writings. Every page of the first edition of his now classic *Basic Satori,* for instance, is entirely devoid of type because the publishers, though scrupulous in their attention to every other detail concerning the preparation of the book—the pagination is flawless, the binding outstanding—completely forgot to include the copy! It's interesting to note that this did not prevent the book from instantly selling out, nor did it deter the leading critics (the review copies were also devoid of any printed matter except for that necessary to establish copyright) from praising it as being "humbling" (*Midwestern Yogi*), and "brilliantly obtuse" (*Kwatz*). The publishers, being no fools, ordered their printers to see to it that all future editions were also blank (because of an error, one run actually did contain copy, but, fortunately, nobody noticed).

Of course in a career as rich and varied and packed full of experimentation as the Roshi's, one must expect to encounter a few mistakes, and Tofu's unrelenting search for truth has not been entirely lacking in blunders. His unfortunate attempts to instruct his students to surpass the full lotus posture by adopting his unique invention of a full lotus and a half led to the many lawsuits from which he has yet to recover; the sharply pointed, pyramidal *zafu* meditation cushions he designed proved so spectacularly uncomfortable that they daunted even the most

TOFU ROSHI

earnest and determined sitters; and the Roshi's essential mis-reading of the famous Ox-Herding Pictures led to serious dis-putes with his Vermont farmer neighbors, which eventually forced the closing of his mountain *zendo*. It is possible that these gentle dairy folk might have forgiven him all the rest, but when the Roshi persisted in loudly and repeatedly shouting "Mu!" at them when they came to reclaim their stolen cows, they misinterpreted his actions and came to the conclusion that he was mocking their simple way of life on top of every-thing else.

In closing, it may be truly said of Tofu Roshi that he, more than any other practitioner of Zen, is himself the greatest living evidence that "Form is emptiness, the very emptiness is form." No matter how you approach him, you will find yourself con-tinuing on in the same direction, unimpeded by any recollection of encounter. Is it Ch'ao Shih Chien who wrote:

> Several birds wanting the same branch.
> A cherry blossom dropped halfway down.
> I forget what I was trying to say.

or someone else?

Speaking of that sort of thing, I haven't the vaguest idea why I sat down to write this, whatever it is, but it's certainly been a pleasant way to pass the time, and I'm enjoying watching the

bright, cheery little letters scroll across the screen.
Besides, it's given me a chance to wish you a nice day.

Gahan Wilson

FOREWORD

INTRODUCTION

I first met Tofu Roshi in traffic school in 1975. The United States had pulled out of Vietnam, and I was casting about for a spiritual discipline, on the lookout for a true teacher. Like many sixties activists, I had come to feel that an important element was missing from my political analysis, indeed, from my life. I felt hollow inside, and the emptiness within was matched by the yawning void without. Friends took me here and there to various spiritual groups they belonged to. I tried Transcendental Meditation, the Sufi Dancing Society, primal therapy, the Hare Krishnas, Scientology . . . but none of these teachings spoke to me personally. The emptiness remained, cloudy and vertiginous, and I became increasingly disconsolate, to the point where I turned right at a red light without coming to a full stop.

Tofu Roshi was in traffic school for going the wrong way on a one-way street. "There is no one way," he told the instructor. I didn't know he was a Buddhist priest at the time—he was dressed in coveralls, with a red wool cap pulled down over his shaved head. But during our lunch break I was struck by the fact that he bowed to his peanut-butter-and-jelly sandwich. And he had extraordinarily pendulous earlobes, that dangled down and swung back and forth when he bowed. I supposed he was another one of Berkeley's marginal people, barely keeping his act together on the outskirts of society.

I forgot about this nondescript man—nondescript except for the earlobes—until I saw him again at a coed dancersize class at the Y. He was the only man in the class (or so I thought), which made a good impression on me, as it indicated a certain freedom from traditional sex roles on his part. This time I saw that his head was shaved. He greeted me with the injunction, "Drive carefully!"

"How many ways to go on a one-way street?" I responded. He laughed and held up one finger, as if testing the wind direction.

He moved with remarkable grace, for one so pudgy, and he hummed along with Donna Summer as we did our leg lifts. When we parted at the door of the Y, he shouted after me, "Not two!" But I never returned to the dancersize class, because the music was not conducive to my spiritual development, and I still didn't know who he was.

The third time I saw him was some months later, at the Next-to-Godliness Laundromat. He was folding his clean laundry into three piles: brown, gray, and black. He smiled at me when I came in. "Keeping in shape?" he asked. Things had been going from bad to worse for me, I was overcome with a sense of meaninglessness, and had come to the laundromat in a distracted state of mind, looking for lost socks. Consequently, I didn't recognize him. I thought a strange man was making a pass

TOFU ROSHI

at me, and I didn't answer. A few moments later, I pulled my head out of a dryer in time to see him leaving the laundromat, his telltale earlobes swaying to and fro. I ran outside and caught up with him at the corner. "I'm sorry," I panted, "I didn't recognize you at first. I keep losing my socks!" As if this would somehow explain my rudeness. "Do you live around here?"

"No way," he nodded. "I'm the priest at the No Way Zen Center up the street. Would you like to join us for the afternoon meditation?"

And so began my new life. I was quickly caught up in the rigors of Zen practice, guided and inspired by the teachings of Tofu Roshi. I will never forget the first dharma talk I heard him give, on "How to Give Up Self-Improvement." A week later, when he spoke on "The Miracle of Mediocrity," I knew I had found my perfect master. In a matter of months, I became one of the dozen residents at the No Way Zen Center, quit my job at the meatless pemmican factory, and began to work as Tofu Roshi's secretary and gal Friday. You will read about these events in the pages that follow.

It was I who persuaded Tofu Roshi to start a spiritual advice column in our local newspaper, to answer the needs of those desperate seekers after truth who struggle alone in the dark, with no one to turn to. It was clear to me that although Tofu Roshi's own training was in the Soto Zen tradition, the breadth of his understanding encompassed the problems encountered in a wide variety of spiritual disciplines.

We have become very close over the years, as close as we could get without overstepping the bounds of propriety. In an era marked by infamous abuses of the teacher-student relationship, Tofu Roshi has never taken advantage of his authority as my spiritual guide. No-self has merged with no-self, but our physical bodies have never touched below the neck, except for the time I accidentally tripped him by stepping on his untied shoelaces, and we fell into each other's arms in the bicycle shed.

The personal biography of Tofu Roshi remains an enigma. Some say he trained as a monk at Tresco Abbey, on the Isles of Scilly, before he opened the No Way Zen Center in Berkeley. His ethnic background is unknown—sometimes he looks Japanese, sometimes like a Russian Jew, and a moment later, in another light, he reminds me of an Irish housekeeper who used to work for my grandmother. He speaks English without an accent, but his usage is somewhat archaic, as if he learned it a hundred years ago. At least one member of our community believes he is a woman, and although I did see him that time in dancersize class, he was wearing such a loose-fitting sweatsuit that I can't refute this theory. Another faction is convinced that the real Tofu Roshi is dead, and that we have as our teacher a skillful impersonator. This brings up the question of who the imposter really is, and, by extension, who is replacing and impersonating the imposter in the gap he left behind. But in the long run, such distinctions are of no importance.

Tofu Roshi is a pure person, of whichever gender, who lives, by and large, in the unconditioned realm of the absolute. As his gal Friday, it has been my role and my privilege to keep him abreast of the times, to read the newspaper for him, and to explain some of the more mundane and contemporary references contained in the letters he receives. His column has now become so well known that he is unable to write a personal reply to every query. As a matter of fact, his teaching responsibilities now take him beyond the gate of the No Way Zen Center into the workaday world of ordinary people, and I have been left in charge of the advice column myself. Up to the present time, however, Tofu Roshi himself has authored the answers that appeared in print, and I have simply taken dictation. To tell the truth, I'm not entirely sure he knows how to read and write, or even how to tie his shoes. On the rare occasion when he needs to wear shoes with laces, he finds some pretext to have me tie them, or else he lets the laces drag along behind. His jealous detractors have made the vicious claim that he became a Zen master because it's one of the few occupations suited to a person who can't read, write, or tie shoes. But a disciple of the Buddha must ignore such idle gossip.

As mentioned above, Tofu Roshi's concern for all sentient

beings, not just Zen students, now keeps him away from the Zen Center most of the time. The spiritual advice column which has succored so many for so long is now in transition. This seems, therefore, the appropriate time to bring together in one volume a selection of letters that we believe speak to the everyday needs of ordinary Americans as they stumble toward satori. It is thanks to Tofu Roshi, and others of his ilk, that Buddhism is taking deep root in the soil of the American mind.

I have grouped the letters into seven chapters, according to their subject matter. I begin each section with some remarks about my own experience as Tofu Roshi's student. These personal comments form a chronological narrative that weaves its way through the book. It is my hope that the history of our own very special teacher-student relationship will serve to put the letters into the larger and richly textured context that is the fabric of Tofu Roshi's life, that net of Indra in which we are all caught like shiny little fishes.

Tofu Roshi and I would like to give special thanks to the following people, who have acted as our advisors for the letters column and whose compassionate understanding, like a deep well, has borne fruit every time we have consulted it: Zea Morvitz, Ron Nestor, Bob Poulsen, Henri Picciotto, Maylie Scott, and Emily Sell.

Susan Ichi Su Moon
No Way Zen Center, 1988

1. HOW TO MEDITATE

"I seem to exhale more completely than I inhale."

In this first chapter, Roshi answers some of the common questions people have about problems they face during meditation. Beginners, of course, have basic questions about meditation practice, such as, "Can you do it lying on your back with your eyes closed?" Furthermore, old-timers may make habitual errors of posture or concentration, or encounter more subtle problems, such as the alarming sensation of turning into a fresh vegetable, and it is important for them, too, to receive corrective instruction. The landscape of meditation is full of pitfalls for both body and mind. Sometimes it's the body that tumbles in, sometimes the mind, and in the letters that follow, Tofu Roshi pulls them out.

In Zen Buddhism, we call our kind of meditation "zazen," and at the No Way Zen Center, newcomers are required to take instruction in how to sit zazen correctly before they are allowed to come to a regular forty-minute meditation period. How well I remember my own first zazen instruction, given to me by Tofu Roshi himself, on that fateful day when I met him at the laundromat, the day I found my teacher but not my socks! It is my hope that others will learn from my experience.

I must preface my story with the reminder that I was in an unstable frame of mind at the time. In my search for spiritual guidance, my hopes had been raised and dashed, raised and dashed again, like a volleyball repeatedly spiked over the net of Indra. But something about this simple man—perhaps that he folded his own laundry—led me to hope once more. Yet even as I hoped, I expected my hope to be shattered, like a basketball that teeters a long moment on the rim, only to fall outside the Hoop of True Understanding.

My heart was already beating, as we walked together from the laundromat to the Zen Center. I took off my brand new Birkenstock sandals, placed them on a beautiful rosewood shoe rack, and followed Tofu Roshi into the zendo. We were alone together, our feet completely bare, in the semidarkness of a hot summer afternoon. The only light filtered in through high and narrow clerestory windows. The air was thickened by the dusky fragrance of roses on the altar. Feeling as afraid, excited and shy as a new bride, I sat down on a round black cushion, which I later learned to call a zafu. I saw beads of sweat on the Zen master's brow, and then I heard him tell me to unfasten my belt and unbutton my pants! For a brief moment, I sat paralyzed, shocked by the lust that had reared its ugly head, while the sounds of cats in heat drifted lazily in on the summer breeze. One part of me even wanted to do it! But all at once I returned to my senses: I leapt to my feet and grabbed a big, flat wooden stick that was lying on the altar. "I've heard about teachers like you," I shouted, brandishing the stick. "You're not going to take advantage of me! I know which side my bread is buttered on, and I'm not making any sandwiches in here with you." I jabbed the stick threateningly at the air as if I had just come up to bat. I had been on the girls' softball team in high school.

"You have the heart of a lioness," said Tofu Roshi in a gentle voice, "and soon we will teach you the use of the stick. In the meantime, please understand that the reason we ask people to unfasten their belts is to facilitate deep and relaxed breathing. It has nothing to do with either sex or baseball. In the zendo, there are no white socks or red socks.

"Compose yourself, and when you are ready for zazen instruction," he continued, "come and get me from the compost heap," and he left me alone in the zendo, waving the stick at the empty air. I hit a couple of line drives into right field, replaced the stick, and sat down to weep with humiliation. Again I heard cats, fighting or mating, and in between their howls of desire, a rhythmic grating that must have been Tofu Roshi's shovel in the compost heap. A voice began to hum a familiar tune—what was it?—and then suddenly burst out into full song: "Six little ducks that I once knew . . ." I wiped my tears with my sleeve, and rose to my feet.

Much later, I came to understand my hysterical response in a different way. Self-knowledge is a frightening thing. On the verge of self-discovery, I was brandishing that stick not, as I thought, at Tofu Roshi, but at my own buddha nature. I was brandishing the stick at deep breathing, at seeing things as they are, at becoming buddha—even at Buddha himself. If I was going to meet Buddha in there, I wanted him to know he couldn't strike me out.

I found Tofu Roshi in the compost heap, and we returned to the zendo, I with my tail between my legs. In this subdued frame of mind I had my first experience of zazen. I sat down opposite Tofu Roshi, and he winked at me and smiled encouragement when, without being told, I loosened my belt. With considerable pain and difficulty, I was able to twist my legs into half lotus, according to his instructions. "Here goes," I said to myself, and I began to breathe. I wanted enlightenment, and I wanted it quick. But I was engulfed by wave after pounding wave of excruciating pain, and after what seemed like ten thousand kalpas, but was probably more like five, I tipped over. I lay on my back like an overturned turtle, my hands still in their mudra, my eyes still cast down at a forty-five-degree angle, which now meant that my gaze fell precisely on a fluffy cloud in the blue sky beyond the clerestory window. And as I lay there, sitting zazen in a supine position, my spirit soared far above and beyond my lumpish body, and melted into the whiteness of the cloud like a pat of butter on a scoop of mashed potatoes. This was it, *It*—nirvana! Surely I'd transcended the wheel of karma and awakened at last on the other shore.

My pleasant reverie was interrupted by the voice of Tofu Roshi, telling me that my zazen posture was excellent in every respect, except that my spine was supposed to be vertical. He slipped that same flat stick under my back and levered me into an upright position—so *that*'s what the stick was for!—and my eyes again took in the knotholes in the floor, which now shimmered with an immeasurable beauty, and twined together like the rings of the Budweiser logo.

"Tofu Roshi," I whispered, "I think I just had enlightenment."

When a Zen student believes he or she has had a true Awakening, the experience must be verified in an interview with a Zen master. The procedure is rather like an oral exam—not the kind you have at the dentist, but the kind you have for your Ph.D. The teacher probes the student's new understanding, looking for depth, sincerity, extinction of the self, and the ability to cite references. I later learned that it is most unusual for a person to attain enlightenment during zazen instruction. In fact, I would have been the first in all the annals of Buddhism.

No—I had not experienced the Great Awakening. Tofu Roshi examined me then and there, and determined that my experience had been one of *makyo*—a delusional hallucination not to be mistaken for true enlightenment, and, in my case, identified as such by my allusion to potatoes. Looking back, I shudder at my ignorance. But Tofu Roshi has taught me to forgive myself. Where do we begin, if not with our own ignorance?

Although I had not achieved unsurpassed complete perfect enlightenment, I had gotten a delicious foretaste of it. I felt a special bond of intimacy with Tofu Roshi, and I knew that it was karma that had brought me to the No Way Zen Center. But when I left the zendo, my new Birkenstocks had mysteriously disappeared from the shoe rack, and I returned home barefoot from the journey that had begun as a search for socks. Thus it was with a mixture of enthusiasm and the hope of finding my sandals that I returned the next day to sit zazen, and the next day, and the next. It was years before I found the sandals. Perhaps if I had found them sooner I would not have progressed as far as I did on the spiritual path.

I tell my own story by way of advising you, if you are a beginner, not to be dismayed by unfamiliar sensations when you meditate. Secondly, do not hesitate to loosen your pants at the waist. As long as you keep them on, you can't get pregnant while meditating, even if you are a woman.

TOFU ROSHI

Dear Tofu Roshi:

When I meditate, I seem to exhale more completely than I inhale, and consequently, by the end of the meditation period, I feel quite deflated. What do you think I should do?

—Prudence Birdwhistle

Dear Prudence:

Proper breathing technique is widely misunderstood. You are not alone in having trouble with it. From your letter it sounds as though you may be making a common mistake: breathing out more times than you are breathing in. This is why we recommend counting breaths. Only by counting can you be completely sure you are exhaling and inhaling the same number of times. One of my students uses golf counters for this. With her left hand she enumerates inhalations, while with her right she takes account of exhalations. At the end of the period, she checks to make sure the numbers on the two counters are the same. If there is any discrepancy, she takes an extra moment to even things up, adding the indicated number of exhalations or inhalations. But it is best to alternate, whenever possible. Breathe in once, breathe out once, and then go all the way back to the beginning of the cycle and repeat. This is a basic principle of Zen.

Dear Tofu Roshi:

Every time I sit down to meditate, the song "Found a Pea-nut" starts running through my head. Is there any help for me? I'm going nuts.

—Georgia

Dear Georgia:

Every song is a sutra, every melody's a mantra, as far as Buddha is concerned. Chant this song as part of your daily service, immediately following the Heart Sutra. Use the lovely Japanese translation, which you will find in the comprehensive and scholarly collection Campfire Sutras.

Dear Tofu Roshi:

When I meditate, I am very distracted by uncomfortable physical sensations, and I seem to spend the whole time fighting off feelings of hunger, sleepiness, or pain. Please help me to regain true focus.

—Bill

Dear Bill:

Let yourself be one with whatever happens in your body. Learn to notice the precise details of your sensations. A good time to practice this is when you eat. How does the feel of the broccoli in your mouth change as you chew? Become *the* warm green softness as it oozes around the gums and tongue.

Do not make assumptions about how you feel. Do not jump to conclusions. Do not name your sensations good or bad. Wait and observe. Do not say to yourself, "I'm hungry, I'm in pain, a scorpion is stinging my left foot." Just be one with the sensations: "heat, tingling, piercing, burning, swelling of the toes . . ." without changing them into ideas. And remember, whatever your experience, it is purely neurological. The sensations themselves actually occur above the neck, between the ears, below the bald or hairy pate. Perhaps, beyond the confines of your skull, nothing else is happening at all!

Dear Tofu Roshi:
   I am troubled by flatulence during meditation.

                                                        —Bart

Dear Bart:
   In what way does this trouble visit you? If it is your flatulence, remember, like everything else, it will pass. While you are about it, you could count these exhalations, also. If it is your neighbor's flatulence, tell yourself that when one farts, all sentient beings fart, with no distinctions, no discriminations. If

your trouble with flatulence is theoretical, then stop worrying about it. It is not an issue of much spiritual significance.

Dear Tofu Roshi:

I am a busy homemaker and single mom of four bouncing boys. For several years now I have been getting up every morning at five, to sit zazen. This has changed my life. During my morning meditation, I am able to do my menu planning, make a mental shopping list, figure out which children will have their baths that night, whose turn it is to take out the garbage, and what color the living-room curtains will be. It's a real great time to work out positive approaches to family problems. Thanks to zazen, my family life has improved tremendously. We have planned-for together time, and my children are clean and well nourished.

Until recently. But now something is going very wrong. Lately when I sit down to meditate, my mind goes completely blank. I can't seem to concentrate on the ingredients of a tuna casserole. I become forgetful of the future and find myself paying attention only to the most trivial things, like the tickly feeling I get in my nostrils from the air passing in and out. Sometimes I even get this weird dizzy feeling, and forget who I am. Nothing seems to have any particular meaning any more. Am I losing my mind?

—Spaced-Out Mom

TOFU ROSHI

Dear Mom:

Deep splendor is nothing special, and that is why you have not recognized it. But many people would give their eye teeth for that tickly feeling in the nostrils.

Dear Tofu Roshi:

I'm a professor of neurophysiology at Harvard Medical School, and I'm very concerned about a colleague of mine who has taken up with a vengeance the practice of what he calls "zazen" and what I call "hyperneuro-oxidation." The human brain is constructed to function properly when a certain proportion of oxygen is present in the blood. We know from studies of mountaineers and nomadic peoples who live at high altitudes where there is less oxygen present that there are severely deleterious effects on the brain from lack of oxygen: in the higher elevations of the Himalayas, for example, almost nobody is able to spell correctly. Now we are beginning to get the results of studies which indicate that an overabundance of oxygen to the brain may be as dangerous as an insufficiency. I urge you, in good conscience, to warn your readers of this hazard. It is my understanding that zazen involves prolonged deep breathing—hyperneuro-oxidation, that is to say—of exactly the sort that is likely to cause brain damage. Surely it is your responsibility to warn people that zazen may render them unable to distinguish right from left, and may cause them to suffer from attacks of narcolepsy during professional meetings, as in the case of my colleague. Some researchers believe that eye-hand coordination is affected, so that it may become difficult for the frequent practitioner to perform such tasks as the tying of shoelaces. There may be a host of other side effects as yet unknown.

—*Dr. John James*

Dear John:

We learn something new every day. Do you not find it remarkable that in spite of the fact that zazen has been causing hyperneuro-oxidation for thousands of years, people still like to do it? Actually, I do not believe it is important to be able to distinguish right from left, because when you come right down to it, one is virtually the same as the other. That is to say, if you were to put them side by side, they would be identical.

Dear Tofu Roshi:

I am easily distracted by noises while I am sitting zazen. The other morning, somebody was trying to start a car just outside the zendo window.

Sixty-three times they tried! The few times the engine actu-

ally turned over, it seemed as though the whole zendo held its collective breath, until the engine would die again. I came out of there a nervous wreck, and arrived at work grinding my teeth and cracking my knuckles. My boss said, "You seem a little tense. Why don't you take up meditation?" How can I achieve inner peace?

—Distractible

Dear Distractible:
   It has been said that the birdsong outside the zendo window will not disturb us when we understand that we are the bird and the bird is us. We face, admittedly, a greater challenge in becoming one with the car that will not start.
   Think of your arms and legs as wheels, your eyes as head-lights, your belly, or hara, as a carburetor. The zabuton on which you sit should extend two inches beyond the rim of the rear tires. Rest the left front hubcap gently on the right front hubcap.

Dear Tofu Roshi:
   When I meditate, the muscles of my right leg twitch invol-untarily and my knee thumps. It's very embarrassing, and there's nothing I can do to control it.

—Twitcher

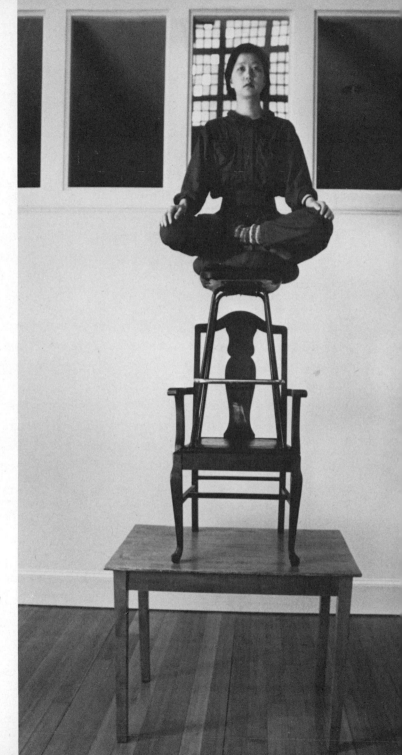

"If you are sitting on a stool which is sitting on a chair which is sitting on a table on the floor, you are sitting on the floor."

Dear Twitcher:

Mild twitches like yours are extremely common during meditative practice. There is a long and respected tradition of neurological dysfunction when in a state of samadhi. How do you suppose the Quakers and Shakers got their names? And in the Eastern tradition, we have the case of Master Fu Shu, whose hands of their own accord assumed the unique thumbwrestling mudra, and battled each other. Then there was the Tibetan priestess, Sihs Bu Mbang, who was subject to seizures of the arms and larynx, such that during deep meditation she would beat her chest with her fists and chant, "Boomalacka, boomalacka, make 'em pay!" at irregular intervals. You have nothing to be ashamed of.

Dear Tofu Roshi:

I can't sit on the floor. I understand that my spiritual advancement is therefore severely hampered. What to do?

—*Stiff*

Dear Stiff:

Many people share your difficulty. Those who begin to practice the Way late in life find it particularly difficult to tie their legs in knots. Some young people who are abnormally "uptight" also have trouble.

You might find it helpful initially to practice your knots on a length of rope. All of us should know the square knot, clove hitch, inside clinch, double carrick bend and studding sail halyard bend anyway. When you can do these knots with the rope, transfer the learning to your legs.

Another approach is an architectural one. Cut a footwell in your floor, which will beautify your home at the same time that it will enable you to sit comfortably on the floor.

Do your best, and remember this: If you are sitting on a chair and the chair is on the floor, you are sitting on the floor. We can even say, if you are sitting on a stool which is sitting on a chair which is sitting on a table on the floor, you are sitting on the floor. Be careful not to fall off the floor.

Dear Tofu Roshi:

Every time I sit sesshin, I am overcome with the desire to go out for ice cream. In between sesshins I don't think much about it.

There is an excellent ice cream store around the corner from our zendo, just five minutes' walk away. And during sesshin we have a break for twenty minutes after each meal. So last sesshin, I planned it all out.

During early morning zazen I thought about a caramel sundae with rocky road ice cream. I continued to think about it all during our breakfast of rice cereal, seaweed and carrots, and fermented bean curd.

When the break came, I set out for the ice cream store, gazing casually at the sky and trying to look as though I was just seeing things as they are. The ice cream store, which is also a coffee shop, was really crowded with people out for Saturday morning breakfast. I ordered my sundae and told them to hold the maraschino cherry. By the time I got served, I had about three minutes to eat my sundae. I must say, it was really delicious, even though I got caramel sauce on my robe, and people looked at me funny.

I hurried through the door of the zendo a few minutes late, trying to look as though I was enjoying my breathing, and when I reached my place, there on top of my zafu was a maraschino cherry. What does this mean? I felt so embarrassed I hid it in the fold of the sutra card.

—Sue Ann

Dear Sue Ann:

Why didn't you sit on it? What is a maraschino cherry but a tiny red zafu? Buddha is everywhere.

2. PROPER FORM
AND RITUAL

"A tangle of used dental floss was stuck to the bottom of my sock."

Zen practice is known for being heavy on form and ritual, and shares with other Eastern religions a great respect for tradition and authority. Many Americans have trouble with this, and have a vague feeling that bowing, for example, is against the Constitution. I checked this out with the American Civil Liberties Union, and learned that the right to bow is actually guaranteed by the Constitution. No problem here. But when we were told we had to wear long-sleeved shirts in the zendo even on hot days, I felt obliged to remind Tofu Roshi that we are also guaranteed the right to bare arms. It is to his credit that he agreed to change the dress code so that it wouldn't be in violation of our civil rights.

This is a short chapter, but the letters it contains all demonstrate the same genius for adapting Buddhist tradition to American culture. Tofu Roshi is able to tread the tightrope that weaves its way like a sailboat between Scylla and Charybdis, between rigid adherence to an outmoded belief system on the one hand and throwing the baby Buddha out with the bath water on the other hand. Anyone following such an ancient

24

path must find a way to bridge the gap between old and new.

After my close call with enlightenment during zazen instruction, I became a regular attender at the No Way Zen Center. My way of life began to change. I rose at 4:30 every morning. I lost touch with my friends. I fell asleep in the middle of evening activities that had once seemed exciting to me. And the more contact I had with Tofu Roshi, the more respect I had for this unremarkable person. During his lectures, I liked to sit up front, so I could watch his simple face and his decorative earlobes. They reminded me of earrings, made of the very flesh itself, the joint creation of nature and artifice. Perhaps he somehow stretched them at night, while he slept. His face—was it a man's or a woman's?—compelled me. It floated before me, not only in my waking life, but also in my dreams, as I unfastened my pants in the zendo.

I'm not the kind of person to give up all my own autonomy and follow a guru, but there was something so nebulous about Tofu Roshi that I knew he would never harm me. He was too vague and shadowy. He could almost have been a figment of my imagination, a reflection of myself. Sometimes I glanced into the mirror and thought I saw his face in place of my own.

About a month after I began to "practice," I realized that the next step for me was to move into No Way, in order to have the opportunity to probe more deeply into the nature of reality and the reality of nature. About a dozen residents lived in the big brown shingled house next to the zendo, and they were required to follow the schedule of the Zen Center, which meant sitting zazen in the morning and evening, and participating in the daily practice of weeding, sweeping, and removing animal droppings from the yard. I let it be known that as soon as there was an opening, I wanted to move in.

In order to prove my sincerity, I was required to sit alone in the zendo for a whole day, leaving only to use the bathroom. I was still a beginner, and by midday the pain in my knees had become unbearable. Still no glimpse of enlightenment. I did as I had been instructed, and counted my breaths. But instead of counting up to ten and starting again, I decided to keep counting. I promised myself a bathroom break when I got to a thousand, but long before I drew my thousandth breath, a power greater than myself compelled me to lie down on the sweet-smelling tatami mat and go to sleep. I *dreamed* I was sitting zazen, so at least it wasn't a total waste of time. Luckily, the same power woke me up and told me to resume the half-lotus position only moments before Tofu Roshi came in to get me at the end of the day.

A few days later, one of the residents obtained a teaching position at the Kansas City Institute of Applied Philosophy, and I was able to move immediately into my new room, which was definitely not as small as a shoe box. I shared a separate apartment at the back of the house with another resident, one of the oldest students at No Way—not in age, but in experience. As Overseer of the Shoe Rack, he held a position of great responsibility at the Zen Center. His name was Shusansaki, and he was a serious and orderly man. He had, for example, hand-calligraphed a sign on the refrigerator that read, "A disciple of the Buddha never refrigerates bananas." And over the toilet a sign said, "Exert meticulous effort here."

I hoped that Shusansaki's influence would help me to become more mindful, perhaps even to keep better track of my socks and shoes. Socks continued to sneak silently away from me, like the fog, on their little cat feet. And I had recently lost a pair of expensive aerobics shoes, I thought from the shoe rack, but I couldn't swear to it. I mentioned this to Shusansaki, and he said he would tighten security around the shoe rack. All in all, I was excited about my new commitment. At last my life would have a central focus.

After I was all moved in, I invited Tofu Roshi over for a cup of Almond Sunset tea and some meatless pemmican. I still worked at the pemmican factory, stirring sunflower seeds into vats of molasses to make a high protein survival food. Our product caused gas, but I knew from observation that Tofu Roshi wasn't afraid of gas. He left his shoes at the door, we sat together on the edge of my bed, which was my only piece of furniture at the time, and I told him how happy I was to be living there, that I was looking forward to getting to know myself, as well as him, in a deeper way. I told him I wanted to go beyond the boundaries of myself, and the boundaries of himself, to the place where we are all one.

By way of conversation, I asked him where he came from. "Why do you want to know? What do you think will be my answer?" he replied.

"Teaneck, New Jersey?" I offered.

"No, I came from the other shore," he said.

"The Jersey shore?"

"The other side. The same place you came from. The place we will both be going."

So then I asked him how he happened to get interested in Zen Buddhism in the first place. "Hah!" he exclaimed. "Who says I'm interested in it? Nothing is interesting. Everything is boring, if you study it closely enough. Don't you find me boring? I find you boring." He smiled sweetly as he spoke.

I choked back the tears. Maybe he meant I bore into the very heart of things. I changed the subject. "Have you ever been married?"

"Everyone is married at some level. Some people are born married, some achieve marriage, and some have marriage

T O F U   R O S H I

thrust upon them. I was born married, and have remained so all my life. One could even say that you and I are married. After all, have we not been to the laundromat together?"

"Do you mean the relationship between a teacher and student is like a marriage?" I asked, getting worried about the implications of this analogy. Was he going to try to seduce me? Or ask me to darn his socks?

"No, my dear Susan," he replied. "I only mean that you and I are not two separate people. That is an optical illusion. We are joined together at the abdomen by our buddha nature, like Siamese twins.

"And now, I must to the dentist," he said abruptly. I was taken aback. You don't think of Zen masters as having to concern themselves with oral hygiene, but, as I later learned, this was one of Tofu Roshi's favorite subjects. "Could you do me a favor and tie my shoes?" he asked shyly. "I hurt my back yesterday in the compost heap, and I am unable to genuflect. And I do not think I should wear flip-flops to the dentist, do you?" I was happy for this opportunity to come a little closer to Tofu Roshi, especially since my efforts to get some biographical information out of him had utterly failed

This was the first time I tied his shoes, but it wasn't to be the last. His shoes were a freshly polished pair of Oxfords, in which, as I knelt before him, I saw my face reflected, and reflected again. As I fumbled nervously with the laces, he began to chant:

> We pay homage to the cobbler,
> We pay homage to the cow.
> We pay homage to the one who ties the bow.
> Their efforts protect the soles of our feet.
> The right foot walks north, the left foot walks south.
> All roads lead to the dentist.

A moment later he was gone.

This was one of the ways in which Tofu Roshi skillfully accomplished the integration of Buddhist form and ritual with our everyday lives. He composed many such verses of praise, called *gathas* in Buddhism—verses suited to particular occasions, rather like the Buddhist version of the verses you find inside greeting cards: "This card from Auntie comes your way, to bring you birthday fun today." His understanding was not culture-bound. With skillful means, he united the old and the new, the Asian and the American, and in this way he constantly supported us in a demanding discipline.

An aspect of Zen practice that is difficult for Americans, and particularly Californians, to accept is the pain in the knees that so often accompanies zazen, and the idea that one should not move, not try to get away from it, but simply accept it. In California, you are supposed to do what feels good. In some parts of the United States, like New York and Boston, suffering comes more easily to the inhabitants, but even there, the tradition tends to be one of mental rather than physical anguish. Tofu Roshi worked patiently to teach us that even in America, even in California, life is suffering, whether you know it or not. You're suffering when you have pain in your knees, and you're suffering when you think you're having fun. He made up a chant for us:

> I accept the pain that visits my knees
> Like hummingbird to honeysuckle.
> We suffer no matter what state we are in,
> Including California.
> Sitting is suffering, surfing is suffering.
> With all beings, we accept our pain.

Halfway through a *sesshin* (a long meditation retreat), when my knees were feeling exactly like honeysuckle flowers being pierced by the sharp bill of a hummingbird, it was very comforting to chant this chant together with my fellow sufferers.

Tofu Roshi teaches that there are limitless possibilities for making form and ritual our own. When I moved into No Way, I began to see his gathas everywhere, written on cards and tacked to the wall: above the toaster, beside the telephone-answering machine, in the bicycle shed, over the shoe rack. Slowly I came to understand that no activity was outside the realm of Buddhist practice. Once I happened to mention to Tofu Roshi that I couldn't get myself into the habit of using dental floss every day, and he said a good Buddhist flosses daily. I said I didn't see what flossing had to do with Buddhism, and so he assigned me the task of making up a gatha to say before flossing. This is what I came up with:

> My mouth is like a Greek temple,
> My teeth the caryatids.
> My mouth is like a Waring blender,
> My teeth the spinning blades.
> With all beings, I take up waxen twine
> To make these blades and columns shine.

Tofu Roshi was delighted. The gatha turned out to be very helpful for me and for my flossing practice, and my dental hygienist, who knew nothing about Buddhism, liked it too, except for the word association she couldn't help making between caryatids and caries. She persuaded me to change "caryatids" to "fluted columns," and then she posted it on her bulletin board to inspire the other recalcitrant flossers among her patients. I recommend making up your own gathas about those aspects of your everyday life that give you trouble. They don't need to rhyme, or have any special rhythm, but they should be brief, and if you throw in the phrase "with all beings," it gives it a truly Buddhist tone.

I was happy at first in my new home, happy at the sound of the wake-up bell, happy at the sound of Tofu Roshi's footsteps, as he shuffled along the corridor to my door, to get his laces tied if his back was bad, or to get my feedback on a new gatha. I could tell that he had a special feeling for me, and I came to believe that his comment about boredom had been made to protect both himself and me from the intensity of his true feelings. At last I was walking on the spiritual path. My world was shrinking, but I was growing. I felt like an opening flower, whose footsteps were following the form and ritual of an ancient tradition that was now perfectly adapted to the life of a young woman in Northern California.

"Dear Tofu Roshi: I can't get my dog to stay on his meditation cushion."

Dear Tofu Roshi:

I can't get my dog to stay on his meditation cushion. Could I just tie the zafu onto the dog for forty minutes a day?

—Doggoned

Dear Doggoned:

When your dog won't sit, which should you tie, the dog or the zafu? Practicing with this question will teach your dog the meaning of shikan taza: Sit! Just sit!

Dear Tofu Roshi:

Our meditation center is being torn apart by acrimonious debate about the proper ritual to follow for leaving the meditation hall. Some say those nearest the door should go first, while others firmly believe that according to the dharma, those furthest from the door but nearest to the altar should go first. In order to save our community, we have agreed to abide by your instructions.

—Waiting on the Truth

Dear Waiting:

People should leave two by two, in order of height, starting with the tallest. Keep a measuring tape by the door in case of uncertainty. Each departing pair should first bow to the altar and then proceed to the doorway to form an arch with their arms, holding it until the second couple ducks under on their way out. The second couple then forms an arch for the third couple, and so on. When everyone has left the meditation hall, all should join together in five minutes of soji, or sweeping of the grounds, while vigorously singing "Turkey in the Straw." In this fashion, we begin the slow work of adapting Asian tradition to American culture.

Dear Tofu Roshi:

I have developed a bad allergy to the smoke of burning incense, and even when I sit at the far end of the zendo from the altar, I am soon choking and coughing uncontrollably. I suppose people have the right to choose to inhale smoke into their own lungs, but they shouldn't impose it on others, especially after they've exhaled it. I don't want their secondhand smoke. Until there is legislation to protect me, how can I continue my practice?

—Incensed

Dear Incensed:

Is there a vestibule or anteroom adjacent to your zendo? If so, install a video camera in the zendo which is focused on the altar, and set up a television in the anteroom with live coverage of burning incense. A surprising number of your sangha members may feel more comfortable bowing to a televised altar. This kind of surveillance is a good security precaution as well and will discourage visiting priests from stealing statues off the altar. If this solution is impracticable, you can always sit zazen in a gas mask, or just hold your breath while you are inside the zendo.

Dear Tofu Roshi:

There's a self-styled feminist who belongs to our Buddhist center, and she's always stirring up a lot of trouble over things like "sexist language" in our chants. She wants us to change all the "he's" to "she or he's," which would be extremely unwieldy and ruin the rhythm, and she (or he) even refuses to accept the fact that Buddha was male. If he was a woman himself, why would he have spent all that time before his enlightenment chasing around after other women? Personally, judging from the way the lady dresses, I think her problem is that she is unable to accept her femininity. She could be reasonably attractive if she would just change to a softer hair style and take off her baggy overalls. If I could get her to do this, I'd feel I was helping her. How do you suggest we deal with her?

—Vive la Difference

Dear Vive la:

Buddha could have been a woman, for all I know. He could even have been a lesbian, though not if he was a man, admittedly. Why do you care? Have you not noticed that in

Buddhist iconography, in contrast to Christian art, Buddha is always depicted without defined sex characteristics? Westerners are obsessed with sexuality, and this tends to get in the way of their enlightenment. Furthermore, the differences between the sexes are grossly exaggerated, as to both degree and complexity. Take my word for it, one sex is very much like another. If you've seen one, you've seen them all.

Dear Tofu Roshi:

I just had a really embarrassing experience. In the middle of our formal silent breakfast in the zendo, I suddenly noticed there was a tangle of used dental floss stuck to the bottom of my sock, just a few inches from my eating bowls, which were spread before me on the mealboard. I had no pocket to slip it into, nothing to do but stare at it helplessly. When the server came around with the miso soup, he noticed it, too. I could tell by the way he paused in front of me, as if frozen for a moment by the terrible sight. His pause attracted the attention of our teacher, sitting nearby, and he saw the floss. Our teacher beckoned the server over, they whispered together, and then the server went to the kitchen. Everybody's eyes were on him when he returned carrying a bowl and salad tongs. After plucking the offending object from my sock, he held it aloft in the bowl, carried it to the altar, and bowed three times to Buddha, while everyone else, following our teacher's example, stopped eating, and held their hands in gassho. I'll never floss again!

—Flossie

Dear Flossie:

Like most of us, you exaggerate the significance of the impression you make on other people. I imagine that by now everyone who witnessed the dental floss incident has forgotten about it completely, or at most they retain a vague impression that you are somehow associated with dental floss and therefore with exemplary methods of oral hygiene.

Looking at the incident from another point of view, you might consider all the different substances people have discovered stuck to the soles of their feet over the course of human history, and you may decide that dental floss, even used, is near the top of the list in terms of desirability.

Do not stop flossing! If dental floss had been available to Shakyamuni, he would have used it, do you not agree? It is time to put the "dental" back in "transcendental."

Dear Tofu Roshi:

My understanding is that in correct oryoki practice we must eat everything in each bowl. At a recent sesshin, a fly landed in my buddha bowl, got stuck, and died there. I picked it up *with my chopsticks and surreptitiously put it under my zafu. Was this the correct thing to do, or should I have eaten it?*

—*J. Goldblum*

Dear J.:

I can see you're one of those people who believe that rules are made for everybody else but themselves, who fly in the face of tradition whenever they feel like it. Of course you should have eaten it, as you said yourself at the beginning of your letter. That fly chose to be born into this life in order to nourish a Zen student. And you chose to be born into this life in order to offer your body as the burial site for a fly. By turning away from this opportunity, you have put off, perhaps by thousands of years, the day when both you and the fly, hand in hand, will escape from the wheel of karma to the other shore, to buzz around from flower to flower, from cube of tofu to cube of tofu.

3. FINDING ONE'S TRUE PATH

"I can't seem to stay with one guru long enough to get enlightened."

In this chapter, Tofu Roshi deals with questions about choosing a spiritual path, and about making a commitment to one's own spiritual development. These are questions dear to my heart, because of the struggle I myself had to pass through before I found my own way to No Way. Even as I sit here on a straw mat in Tofu Roshi's old office, working at the computer on top of which stands the little figure of Manjusri, the "perfect wisdom bodhisattva," even now, so many years later, I am newly grateful for what I have found, and I daily renew my commitment. Through the window drift the familiar sounds of cats fighting and mating, and I see various sangha members flapping about in their flip-flops: weeding, cleaning the yard with the pooper-scooper, hanging the dishtowels up to dry, grinding sesame seeds. It's hard to believe there was ever a time when I didn't know this place, when I didn't know the sound of the wooden clappers or the little zendo bell. Or the sound I hear at this very moment, the grating of a shovel in the compost heap.

Tofu Roshi used to say his own true path led him to the compost heap. It was his great passion to take care of it, to take its temperature, to shovel and sift and strain. Many's the time

I've heard him speak allegorically of the compost heap in his lectures, pointing out how decay is part of life—how the baby carrot hatches out of the dead eggshell. Other times he says the compost heap is an example of how you might think you can leave things be, but everything's always changing and cooking and heating up, whether you want it to or not, just as we are doing on our cushions. He says that the zendo, when we enter it, becomes a great compost heap. He says it might look as though nothing's happening, but left to ourselves on our zafus, we disintegrate and ferment and cook ourselves, and little baby carrots sprout from our ears. He says we need to be turned and aerated, with bowing and chanting and walking meditation, so that we don't get compacted, so that our zafus don't get stuck to our bottoms. Evidently, this actually happened in a monastery in New Jersey, where an overzealous teacher, eager to refute the allegation that Americans are too soft for disciplined Zen practice, had his students sit on their cushions for days at a time with no breaks except to go to the bathroom. Both students and zafus were made of 100 percent organic material, bacterial action was rapid in the heat and humidity of the New Jersey summer, and at the end of the practice period, the students and their zafus had to be surgically separated.

Roshi also says our brains are like a compost heap, that all our thoughts and plans are like various pieces of garbage—a memory is like a banana peel, a fantasy is like a paper cone full of coffee grounds, a future plan is no more than the peelings of a potato—and that with time, if we leave these thoughts alone, they will decompose and turn to rich dark soil in which the dharma can grow.

But I stray from my point. I wish to speak further about my own journey to No Way, and how I came to make my commitment.

It took me months to feel sure that No Way was my way. But even in the first few days, I noticed some immediate and profound changes in myself. Roshi had given me the practice of counting my breaths up to ten. Soon I couldn't stop counting up to ten in my everyday life outside the zendo. I found myself compelled to chew each bite of food ten times, whether it was yogurt or celery, and I felt a rush of satisfaction every time I counted my fingers and toes. There were other early effects. Almost every night I dreamed of Tofu Roshi: barefoot, he carried me across a sea of compost. I was no longer afraid of death, and although I was still afraid of the two biggies—earthquakes and airplanes—I noticed that I was no longer afraid of both of them at the same time, and this I ascribed to my meditative practice.

However, I had a lot of resistance to overcome. I had come

of age in the sixties, and learned, along with the rest of my generation, to question authority. Blind obedience to tradition was not for me. In the seventies, I espoused feminism—I'm not sure whether it was as the husband or the wife—and I worked hard to unlearn the habit of submission to male authority. It had been a long, hard struggle for me, as it was for many of my sisters, to reclaim my own power. Now I wanted a teacher, but I didn't want to give up all my power to Tofu Roshi. How could I reconcile my longing for a teacher with my belief in my own autonomy?

I encountered external resistance to my spiritual development as well. My friends were afraid that I had joined some kind of cult, that I would give away all my earthly possessions, including my oft-borrowed vacuum cleaner. My mother was afraid I would shave my head and thereby give up my chances of meeting a nice man to marry before it was too late to provide her with grandchildren. I reminded her of her refrain to me all through my childhood: "Honey, you have such a pretty face, if only you'd get the hair out of your eyes so I could see it." And I told her that if she wasn't so old-fashioned, she'd know that some men are turned on when women shave parts of the body that aren't usually shaved. That quieted her, momentarily. I didn't give her the satisfaction of admitting that I had no intention of shaving my head. Little did I know . . .

Neither of my parents would come to see me at No Way for the first several months I lived there. My father didn't like the name of the place. He said it demonstrated a negative attitude toward society. My friends from my women's consciousness-raising group wouldn't come because they thought I'd sold out to a male-dominated system. Actually, they became intrigued when I told them that some sangha members believed that Tofu Roshi was without a member—was in fact a woman. After that, two of them came to visit me out of curiosity—they wanted to check out Tofu Roshi's gender. But they went away uncertain, the matter still unresolved, as it was not possible for them to conduct the necessary investigations.

How did I overcome the resistance within and without, and commit myself to a spiritual path? The turning point came one day during dokusan with Tofu Roshi. *Dokusan* is the name for a private interview between teacher and student in which the teacher gives the student guidance about his or her practice. It is confidential, and neither teacher nor student is supposed to speak of what takes place within the walls of the dokusan room. Like a whale, I breach this custom, renouncing privacy, to spout the truth of my experience, in the hope that it will be helpful to others.

I had been living at No Way for about a month. My interest had been deepening, but so had my discomfort at what I found to be a disturbingly authoritarian power structure. That very day, Shusansaki had castigated me for leaving a pair of socks lying around for days on the bottom shelf, the one reserved for the head priest's footwear, that is, for Tofu Roshi. Socks were apparently my Achilles' heel. I was still smarting from his words—"They're all stretched and misshapen!"—when I went into the dokusan room with a chip on my shoulder. The first thing you are supposed to do when you come in the door is bow to the teacher, but it was at that moment impossible for me to bow to Roshi, because of the chip, so I sat straight down on the cushion, my heart in my breast, and waited for his response to my defiance of his authority.

Nothing happened. He sat facing me with downcast eyes, while I listened to the rhythmic buzz of a fly. Would he ask me to leave? To come in again, and do it right? What if he made me polish a brick until I could see my original face reflected in it? The fly's buzz changed to a sort of snuffle, and all at once I knew that this was no fly, but the sound of Tofu Roshi snoring.

I was disappointed. My declaration of independence had fallen on deaf ears, and I might never again have the courage to commit such an act of civil disobedience. What should I do? "Let sleeping dogs lie," I said to myself. Besides, I had always wanted to get a closer look at Tofu Roshi's earlobes, and here was my opportunity. As Roshi's adenoids continued their flylike buzzing, I crouched forward and peered closely at his left ear-lobe—or perhaps it was his right one, I don't recall. The flesh hung soft and heavy, swelling like a teardrop at the bottom.

At that very moment, Roshi awoke with a shudder. I was on my hands and knees, my face just inches from his ear. "Good afternoon, Susan," he said, and bowed to me. "Have you lost something?" He seemed, immediately, to be wide awake.

I retreated to my zafu and began to cry. Spiritual practice is powerful medicine. After a couple of months of practice, my old personality structure was already crumbling. I was confronting all my inner conflict around individuation. I wanted to be taken care of, to belong, to be told what to do, to be subsumed into the black-robed long-lobed body of my teacher. And I wanted to be separate, to step away, not to bow. "I've lost track of who I am," I wailed. "When I came in, I didn't even bow. I don't think it's good for me to submit myself mindlessly to your authority. I need to discover myself, not give away my power! Who am I? Roshi, who am I? Who are you? Why am I here?" My doubt took me right back to square one. I was questioning whether my true path was at No Way, where the authoritarian power structure felt like fingernails going against the grain. "If I have to do one more thing without knowing why, just because you say so, I'm leaving!" I declared. I was having a crisis of faith as profound as Saint Augustine's.

It was then that Tofu Roshi offered me a job as his secretary. "Forget bows!" he said. "When you refuse to bow to me, you refuse to bow to yourself. It is not skin off my teeth!" Suddenly my doubts fell away, like autumn leaves falling from wind-shaken boughs, or chips falling from shoulders. "I need help with my correspondence," he explained, "and with the preparation of my lectures. You have already demonstrated your verbal skill by composing a verse on dental floss. I appreciate your stubborn independence, your resistance to false authority. Let us work together in the dharma!"

Dear Tofu Roshi:

Please help me. I'm so confused—I just can't seem to settle down with one guru and get enlightened.

Five years ago I began meditating with the Swami from Miami, Guru Lethar Ji, a disciple of Swami Prokrastananda of the school of Non-Action. It was easy to follow his path, but I have to say it got boring. Then my roommate, Fred, told me about Selfism. Just out of curiosity, I went to see Selfi Sol, and right away I knew his teaching was for me, myself and I. I practiced Selfism for about a year, but when the length of my own toenails, which I measured every morning according to our practice, became more interesting to me than the daily newspaper, I feared that I was becoming too self-absorbed. At that time, as karma would have it, I happened upon an article in Fulfillment Semi-Monthly *about a Buddhist teacher named Mu Kao Roshi. One visit to his zendo changed my life. In half lotus, I threw myself into my koan study. I drank a lot of milk, and learned to moo like a cow. I almost "got" my koan, you know, the one about Noh Wei and the dirty dishes . . .*

But then one day on the car radio I heard an interview with Baba Bubbahubba, and I just had to keep right on driving until I got to the Bubbahubba Ashram. I shaved my head, gave up my car, and looked only with my third eye.

Since then I've been with Yogi Seemalingam, Siddie Sadie,

Mahaha, and several other Perfect Masters. Each time I think I've found the path and the guru, but after a few months I get this itchy feeling and somehow I just have to move on. Please help me. I know I'm wasting my time and I'll never get enlightened this way.

—Unfaithful in Inverness

Dear Unfaithful:

Don't give up until you have tried the teachings of Tofu Roshi. I suggest you send for my somewhat low-priced booklet, "The Miracle of Mediocrity."

Dear Tofu Roshi:

I'm just fifteen, and last week for the first time I journeyed out of my body and ran away from home. I hate school.

By law I have to go to school until I'm sixteen, but what I need to know is, if my body goes to school without me in it, is it still legal?

—High School Drop-Out

Dear Drop-Out:

I believe the issue has not yet been tested in court, but I support you in your spiritual journey. I caution you, however, not to stay out of your body so long that you are unable to remember how to get back in when the fun begins.

Dear Tofu Roshi:

   I am weird. Can I help it?

—Anonymous

Dear Anon:

   I would have to make your acquaintance before I could answer your question. Were you born weird, or did you later become so?

   In any case, the most important thing is to accept yourself as you are, assuming, of course, that you first take care of your personal grooming and hygiene. Many of the great Buddhist teachers of history were very eccentric individuals. Did you know that the ancient Chinese master, Bush Wak, had the right hand of a woman and the left hand of a man? It is unknown to this day whether Bush Wak was male or female. As for Master Za Phu, he insisted on wearing his eating bowl to bed as a night cap. In cold weather, he wore the cloth case for his eating utensils as a codpiece, after removing the chopsticks, spoon, and setsu stick. I beg you to accept yourself as you are. Buddhist practice is what you may call a "come-as-you-are party."

Dear Tofu Roshi:

   Is there a gourmet guide to spiritual practice places? My wife and I need to know, in choosing our path, where we can get our dietary needs met. I have heard of Zen centers where peanut butter is the mainstay of every meal, but we are more interested in something in the nouvelle cuisine line: radicchio, chanterelles, that sort of thing.

When you give up all your ordinary activities, food becomes even more important than usual, and that's saying something! My wife and I wish to spend our summer vacation on a long retreat. I am overweight, and I hope to lose pounds but gain insights, about twenty of each. My wife, who is very slim, is allergic to wheat and milk. I should perhaps add that neither of us is enthusiastic about the idea of eating seaweed, and we wonder if people have been able to get enlightened without it. One more thing—cooked carrots make me gag. What do you recommend for us?

—Orrie O'Kea

Dear Orrie:

Do not make false distinctions. Food is buddha, we are buddha. When we eat, we eat ourselves. Your hair is seaweed, your legs are carrots. Do you not like your legs? Eat your legs raw. You are what you eat. So is your wife.

Dear Tofu Roshi:

I have recently returned from a yoga retreat with Baba Hari Chin, a monk who has been practicing continual silence ever

"When I asked him how to extinguish greed, he took out his teeth."

since his mother asked him whose muddy footprints were all over her clean carpet.

Every morning we practiced asanas of the seven-limbed soul-path, and then we had a question-and-answer period with Babaji. He never broke his vow of silence, and I am sorry to say that at times I found his answers difficult to understand, and I thought perhaps I just wasn't ready for his teaching. When I asked him how to extinguish greed, for example, he took out his teeth. What did he mean by this?

—Neophyte

Dear Neophyte:

He was telling you not to bite off more than you can chew. He was also demonstrating what can happen to you if you don't floss daily.

Dear Tofu Roshi:

I am worried about my daughter, who has joined an ashram which sounds like some kind of cult to me. She wrote home that they are required to sleep lying down, to meditate and take their meals in a sitting position, and to move about vertically, placing the soles of the hind feet against the floor, and transferring the weight alternately from one to the other. I

TOFU ROSHI

don't mean to be ethnocentric, but this sounds like humiliation of the fiesh to me. Have you heard of these practices?

—Labrador Retriever's Mom

Dear Mom:

Yes, I have heard of kennels where such practices are taught. Though they may seem extreme, I do not believe they are harmful. They provide a new way for us dogs to work on the old koan, "Does a human being have buddha nature?"

4. STAYING ON THE PATH

"How can I get my higher and lower self to cooperate with each other?"

It is one thing to find a spiritual path, and it is another thing to stick to it. The initial excitement experienced by the new convert is all too soon replaced by boredom; the sense of spiritual awakening gives way to the desire to sleep in. In many ashrams, zendos and temples of the spirit, a turnover in membership can be observed that follows a characteristic pattern. There seems to be a watershed somewhere between six months and a year after joining, when the drainage system takes the student east or west from the mountain's ridge. In Buddhism we speak of the gateless gate. Every day we must ring the silent doorbell and step again over the invisible threshhold.

As for me, when I quit my job at the pemmican factory and began to work as Tofu Roshi's secretary, my world was completely circumscribed by the boundaries of the No Way Zen Center. I lived, worked, and exerted meticulous effort there, and nothing took me beyond the gate but my trips to the Next-to-Godliness Laundromat, to feed my socks to the washers and dryers.

My relationship with Shusansaki was becoming increasingly tense, providing us both with an opportunity to overcome anger. He was evidently jealous of me for the intimacy I shared with Tofu Roshi as his secretary and confidante. Once Shusan-saki came upon us beside the shoe rack, as I was bent over Tofu Roshi's feet, tying his new aerobics shoes. Roshi was about to go to dancersize class, but he couldn't tie his shoes because he had blisters on his hands from turning the compost. Shusansaki made a stiff little bow. After Tofu Roshi had left he said to me, "I don't think it's appropriate for you to be tying Roshi's shoes. You're not his mother."

"Would it be more appropriate for me to contact his mother and ask her to come here to tie his shoes?" I asked, feeling anger arising.

"I happen to know that his mother has passed away," declared Shusansaki, "and if anybody is going to tie his shoes, I should be the one to do it. I would have thought it would be clear to you that as Overseer of the Shoe Rack, I'm responsible for all problems in the field of shoes and socks."

"I was only doing what I was asked to do by our teacher," I replied, not without smugness.

Shusansaki laughed. Then he took off his sandals, put one of them on his head, and walked away, keeping the sandal carefully balanced on top of his head, as if he was doing some kind of posture exercise. What a strange guy!

As time went on, I must confess that I, too, came to experience the piercing anguish of boredom, and it was out of this anguish that I suggested to Tofu Roshi that he start a spiritual advice column, in the *No Newsletter*. By sharing the teaching, I hoped to move beyond the boundaries of my own small self—though it was not as small as I wished, particularly at the hips.

In our first column we ran a reprint of Roshi's lecture on "How to Give Up Self-Improvement," and put out the call for letters. We were overwhelmed by the response. In unanticipated numbers, the letters came trickling in. On rainy days our mailbox was full of limp envelopes, and on sunny days the letters were crisp as fresh potato chips. How I loved to pass the mornings with Tofu Roshi in his study, reading the letters out loud to him, taking down his answers as he dictated them. I was not so much the Dorothy to his William Wordsworth, as Boswell to his Johnson, by which I mean to say he treated me with respect and valued my opinion. There were even times when it wasn't completely clear which of us had composed the answer. Through this process, I confronted and worked through many problems which were my own, for at the deepest level we all share the same problems. We sit side by side on our meditation cushions, and whatever stands in the way of your enlightenment stands also in the way of mine. If flatulence is your problem, it is also mine.

In this chapter we have included the letters that deal with the difficulty of sustaining a spiritual discipline over the long haul. Anyone who has tried to keep to a regular meditation schedule for a long period of time has known moments when the flesh rebels, calling out for sleep, sex, or ice cream. And we have also known those dark nights of the soul when the spirit cries out, "No way!"

At No Way, as at most Buddhist centers, we have certain ceremonies to mark these passages, to help the weary hiker stay on trail. After about a year, I knew it was time for me to formally declare my commitment to Zen practice, and I told Tofu Roshi I was ready to have my *jukai* ceremony; that is, to take my vows as a Buddhist, and to receive my Buddhist name. But before the ceremony, I had to sew my *rakusu,* or symbolic robe. This was a long and painstaking process, and the sewing teacher was none other than Shusansaki, a harsh taskmaster if there ever was one.

According to our tradition, this first robe is an abbreviated one, made in the shape of a bib, so that it can be worn during formal meals in the zendo to protect the clothing from spaghetti sauce. Some have compared the difficult piecing together of the little rakusu to traditional Appalachian quilting, or to the making of a latticed crust for strawberry-rhubarb pie. The stitches holding together the seventeen little pieces of cloth have to be exactly $1/16''$ apart, and according to the tradition followed at No Way, the neophyte repeats the mantra

"Unique New York," with the taking of every stitch. *Unique New York, Unique New York, Unique New York.* Just try to say it quickly, nine times in a row.

Shusansaki measured my stitches from time to time. Once he found a stitch that was too long, and he made me resew the whole section. "Aha!" he exclaimed, with ill-concealed satisfaction. "Trying to make it go faster by taking long stitches, are you? Don't you know you can't fool Buddha? He knows how long your stitches are." But at last, after an agony of tangled thread and tangled tongue, my little robe was done, and I was ready to become a Buddhist. I even felt a certain bond with Shusansaki, who had seen me through to the end, and actually expressed some satisfaction with my work.

I invited a handful of friends and relatives to the ceremony. My parents had finally accepted the fact that I was a Buddhist, whether they liked it or not, and that if they wanted to see me they would have to come to No Way, which my father now referred to as the Nosirreebob Zen Center. My non-Buddhist guests settled themselves in chairs, which Tofu Roshi had thoughtfully put out for them at the back of the zendo, except for my mother, who, in a fit of enthusiasm, sat on a zafu and immediately began to fidget, now sticking her legs straight out in front of her, now wrapping her arms around her knees.

At the beginning of the ceremony, Tofu Roshi said that if any

TOFU ROSHI

person present knew of a reason why I should not become a disciple of the Buddha, he should speak now or forever hold his peace.

"I do," said Shusansaki. I could hardly believe my ears. I felt like he'd knocked the wind out of me. Was he going to say that my stitches were too long? "A disciple of the Buddha does not take what is not given," he continued in a leaden voice, "and I have reason to believe that Susan is the person who has been stealing shoes from the shoe rack. Just this morning, a pair of Clark's Wallabies disappeared while she was sweeping off the porch and I was grinding rice in the kitchen." A shocked silence fell like a giant wet blanket over the assembled throng.

Tofu Roshi called an immediate halt to the ceremony, and everybody filed out the door to the shoe rack, whispering to each other. Suddenly a voice cried out, "My Italian sandals are gone! Look, there goes somebody out the gate . . ." I caught sight of a camouflage-patterned sleeve passing behind the princess tree. Determined to catch the culprit and thereby prove my innocence, I first ducked back into the zendo to grab the stick off the altar, and then ran out the gate in pursuit of the urban guerrilla, the one who had stolen my jukai ceremony.

"Stop, thief!" I shouted at a receding figure in a camouflage jumpsuit who was pushing a stroller. There was nobody on the block but the three of us: me, her, and the occupant of the stroller. Nobody to help me catch her. But in my rage, I knew no fear and chased headlong after her, waving the stick. I ran around in front of her and faced her down, my stick raised high. She stopped, and the baby in the stroller began to cry. I looked right at her feet, and was disappointed to see there a pair of green Converse hightops. "Give me back the Italian sandals you just took from the Zen Center shoe rack," I said in a steady voice, looking her right in the eye. "You haven't fooled us with your camouflage suit or your baby."

Well, it turned out she lived nearby, and was only bringing over a letter for the Zen Center that had been erroneously delivered to her address. We got to talking, and discovered that we had lived in the same dorm at college. I invited her over to No Way for zazen instruction, which I now gave on Tuesdays, and she came the very next Tuesday. Her name was Mercy, and she soon became an active member of our community.

But that's another story. I returned to the Zen Center crestfallen, without the stolen shoes, and met with Shusansaki and Tofu Roshi to discuss my case. I pointed out that I could hardly be the shoe thief as the Italian sandals had been stolen while I was inside the zendo waiting to be ordained. Shusansaki actually went so far as to suggest that I could have arranged to have a friend steal the shoes on this occasion, precisely in order to clear myself of suspicion. Naturally I was very upset by his accusations, and I had an impulse to move out of No Way then and there, particularly since I shared an apartment with my accuser. Or at the very least to put bananas in the refrigerator. But Tofu Roshi was convinced of my innocence, and reminded Shusansaki that he had been weeding the garden a few feet away the whole time I was sweeping the porch. Like a parent mediating a fight between siblings, he told Shusansaki to apologize to me. "Sorry I said you stole the shoes, Susan," sighed Shusansaki, staring at his sandals. My ordination ceremony was rescheduled for the following week. How grateful I am now that Tofu Roshi gave me the support I needed to stay on the path through those terrible times.

Again we set up chairs, and again the zendo was filled with sangha members and my invited guests. Tofu Roshi asked the same question as before, and they all turned to look at Shusansaki, holding their collective breath. Nobody said a word. And so, as incense exhaled its pungent smoke into the zendo air and cats howled beyond the windows, I took my vows, put on my bib, and received my Buddhist name from Tofu Roshi. On that day I became Ichi Su, which means either "Morning Thunder" or "Almond Sunset," depending on the context.

We had a little reception afterward in the garden, and even Shusansaki gave me a congratulatory hug. I was looking forward to Tofu Roshi's embrace, which I hoped I had earned at last by my commitment and my careful stitches. As he approached me with a twinkle in his eye, a dog with a zafu tied to its back streaked through the garden, knocking Tofu Roshi over like a bowling pin. He had to lie there resting for the next hour, and he couldn't tie his shoes for two weeks.

As for staying on the path, my experience has taught me that the trail is rocky, and sometimes overgrown with poison oak or ivy. Step around it, but stay on the path. You may think you have lost the way altogether, but if you persist, a spiritual guide like Tofu Roshi is bound to come along sooner or later. After all, nothing ventured, nothing gained, as the saying goes, and furthermore, fools rush in where angels fear to tread.

Dear Tofu Roshi:

How can I get my higher and lower self to cooperate with each other? I am torn apart by conflicting desires. To sleep, or to sit shivering with cold in the early morning dark of the zendo? To make love with my wife, or to go to a class on the Heart Sutra? It's not just a time conflict, but a philosophical conflict as well. The sutra says, "No eyes, no ears, no nose, no tongue, no body, no mind," and this makes lovemaking difficult, if not impossible. I could probably muddle through without the first three, but the other stuff I need.

—Zendoid

Dear Zendoid:

Your dualistic thinking is causing you unnecessary suffering. Stand on your head and ask yourself where is your higher self, where is your lower. Or ask yourself, "Who is it, who makes love with my wife?"

Dear Tofu Roshi:

One aspect of the eightfold path is avoiding idle talk. Could you give us some pointers on how to do this without closing down the lines of communication?

—Gift of Gab

"Stand on your head
and ask yourself
where is your higher
self, where is your
lower."

Dear Gift:

1. *Omit articles, adjectives, adverbial clauses.*
2. *Talk fast. Faster you talk, sooner you silent.*
3. *Remember: If you think you have something of interest to say, you could be wrong. Especially, do not recount your dreams.*

Dear Tofu Roshi:

I am studying Buddhism at a Zen center where the priest shaves his head, and nobody else does. My problem is that I am completely bald. People think that I must be a priest, too, and they act extra holy around me, walking on the balls of their feet and speaking in whispers. Or, what's worse, they think I shave my head in order to be taken for a priest.

Sometimes I wonder if our priest feels jealous of my glistening scalp. His is so whiskery. As my grandfather used to say, "God made a few perfect heads, and the rest he covered with hair."

How can I clear up the confusion? Do you think I should get a hair transplant?

—Bald but Unenlightened

Dear Bald:

I don't think one hair would make much difference. Several would be required, would they not? But it is not necessary.

Do we not say in the sutra, "No eyes, no hairs, no nose, no tongue, no body, no mind?" Do not let small-minded people pull the wool over your eyes.

Dear Tofu Roshi:

I'm desperate. I've been meditating for ten years now, and I still haven't experienced enlightenment. At least I don't think I have. I went to my family doctor for a complete physical checkup, just to make sure there was no physiological problem. He says I'm the picture of health, except for my planter's warts, and he doesn't see why they would stand in the way of enlightenment.

Recently I returned from a month-long meditation retreat. I thought by the time it was over I would surely experience the big E. People were calling out all around me, moaning and exclaiming with transcendent rapture. But I just sat there, trying not to scratch. Roshi, what if they're all faking? What if it's just a big hype? Should I fake satori, too? Then I'd get some respect. But luckily for me, I had a religious upbringing, and I know that if I simulated enlightenment, I wouldn't be cheating anybody but myself.

After the retreat was over, I asked the guy who had been sitting next to me, "Have you had satori?" He replied coolly, "That's a private matter I prefer not to discuss."

TOFU ROSHI

Another time I asked some people in my sangha if they'd be interested in us forming an ongoing support group for pre-satoric beings, but they looked at me like I was suggesting we start a massage class for people with contagious skin disease.

Oh, Roshi, is there really such a thing as Enlightenment? And if there is, why don't I ever have it?

—Virginia

Dear Virginia:

Yes, Virginia, there is Enlightenment. You will know it when you have it. But let me tell you something in confidence. People who do experience satori are often disappointed to discover that their lives are just as dreary afterward as they were before. "No big deal," as they say. When you are en-lightened, you will realize that you already realize that which you will realize when you are enlightened.

Dear Tofu Roshi:

Every day we chant the Heart Sutra. I know this is sup-posed to be the heart of our practice, but it feels bloodless to me, like when I automatically recited the Lord's Prayer in Sunday School. How can I make the Heart Sutra relevant to my life?

—Automatic Pilot

Dear Pilot:

I suggest you form a Heart Sutra Club, as members of our sangha did. Their goal is to amass merit by doing good works, and then to redistribute it among those who have little or none. The group recently went on a field trip to the local blood bank, and donated blood together while chanting the Heart Sutra. I went along, at their request, to ring the bells and lend an air of legitimacy to the occasion. It was both a learning experience for the nurses and an intense bonding experience for the club members, each of whom returned home with a red plastic key tag in the shape of a heart.

Dear Tofu Roshi:

At a long retreat, you get to know people really well in a certain way. You get to know their physical presence, how they walk, and bow, and chew their food, if they do chew.

Well, here is my problem. When I go to a long retreat, instead of becoming more open and loving as the retreat progresses, I become more and more critical of the sentient beings around me. At our last retreat, there was a man who, after each step in walking meditation, would nod his head with satisfaction, as if he was congratulating himself for being so holy. And there was a woman who, when she pressed her palms together to bow, crooked her little fingers as if she was drinking tea at Windsor Castle. At such times, I am choked by rage. I want to break things. I flush with hot anger at every ladylike bow or self-satisfied nod. Did you ever feel this way? In my normal life, I'm a fairly nice person.

—Gladys

Dear Gladys:

Once I had a student who could not stop from plucking tiny woolballs off her sweater all during zazen. She provided us with an opportunity to practice patience and tolerance. One day I noticed with some relief that she had finally rendered her sweater completely threadbare, but she arrived the next day in a new sweater, and began work on it.

About halfway through a long retreat, in order to facilitate the release of tensions such as you describe, I often have the community join together in a sort of modified game of charades, in which each person takes a turn to imitate the irritating foibles of another, while the onlookers guess who is being impersonated. We all feel much closer to each other after our little improvisational theater session.

Dear Tofu Roshi:

Buddhist centers are usually in need of funds, yet fundraising is not a popular activity. I thought it might be helpful, therefore, to share with your readers two fundraising ideas that

*have worked well for us at our Temple of American Shavings
and Bone, a Rinzai monastery.*

*We have always held monthly sesshins, one week long, with
a set price for room and board. Now, every other month, we
make our sesshin a "Cleansing Sesshin," in which we utilize a
reduced intake of food, but keep the price the same. We still
haven't gone the limit on the money-saving possibilities of
these sesshins, and we may decide to go a step or two further,
by limiting people to one slice of pickled radish per day,
cutting the paper napkins in quarters instead of halves, and
changing all the lightbulbs to twenty-five watts, once we figure
out how.*

*Secondly, we scrapped our annual fundraising dinner this
year, always a capital-intensive and labor-intensive affair, and
held our first Zen-a-thon instead. Participating members were
given pledge cards, and asked their sponsors to pledge a
specific donation to Shavings and Bone for every period of
zazen they sat. Sponsors were encouraged to pledge a bonus if
the sitter had kensho. The Zen-a-thon began at our usual time
of 5:00 A.M. on a Monday morning, and continued until the
last participant fell off her zafu. Experience taught us that it
was good karma for people to give their sponsors a rough idea
of how many periods they expected to sit, and whether or not
they expected to have kensho. Some people were cheaper to*

T O F U   R O S H I

sponsor than others, of course. All in all, this nondualistic event was a great success, both financially and spiritually—truly *Zazen in Action*.

I hope these ideas will help others to put the fun in fundraising.

—*An Ascetic Accountant*

5. INTIMATE RELATIONSHIPS

> *"Now he spends all his free time sifting through ashes for stubs of incense."*

One morning as I walked down the hall to his office, I thought I heard Tofu Roshi muttering to himself. Curious, I paused outside the door. "Are you awake?" I heard his familiar voice asking, that voice that was high for a man's, low for a woman's. Could he have somebody sleeping in the office with him?

"Yes, Roshi, I am," came the shocking answer, shocking because I recognized the speaker. And do you know whose voice it was? It was Roshi's own!

The conversation continued. "Would you like another cup of tea?"

"Yes, please, if you don't mind," he answered himself politely. "At your convenience," he added as an afterthought.

I knocked at the door. "Go on in, Ichi Su," I told myself. "Don't stand on ceremony!" A few moments later, Roshi asked me to bring him another cup of tea. "I asked myself to do it," he said, "but apparently I wasn't listening."

In this chapter we include letters about intimacy, or the lack of it, as it pertains to the soul's journey. One of the most frequent problems that comes up is how to reconcile the demands of a spiritual practice with the demands of an intimate relationship, especially when one partner is not on the spiritual path. It is not news that the human being's longing for erotic love, for merging with another sentient being, throws quite a monkey wrench into his or her search for enlightenment. Buddha told us long ago that desire gives rise to suffering. Nevertheless, we all seem to have to learn the hard way.

In my own case, living as a single woman at No Way, and working all day with Tofu Roshi, I had to struggle with my own growing attachment to him. He was the most important person in my life; he was my significant other. I felt incredibly close to him, and yet there was this great distance. We had never so much as hugged each other, and I still didn't know for sure whether he was a man or a woman, although I tended to think of him as a man. Sometimes I wondered whether my love for him would change if I found out he was a woman, and so I periodically gave myself the mental exercise of thinking of him as a woman. I tried to do this for several hours at a time, once a week.

On one of the mornings I'd chosen for Tofu Roshi to be female, we sat together in her office taking a tea break between letters. We were having a conversation about life cycles, wondering whether there is an age at which people are most ready to develop themselves spiritually. At the same time, I was working on a visualization exercise: I was picturing Roshi's soft breasts beneath her shapeless robe—large and round and wide set. "How old were you when you first sat zazen?" she asked me.

"Thirty-four C," I replied, staring at her bosom.

Her glance followed mine to her chest, and she picked a piece of lint off her robe, perhaps thinking that's what I was staring at. Suddenly I was embarrassed, I blushed, I fidgeted. "B," she said. "Just be. As Laotzu said, 'The way to do is to be.'"

"Thirty-four, see what I mean?" I continued, trying to save myself. "See I could have been thirty-three, or thirty-five, but as it happened I was thirty-four." Yes, I loved her on the days when she was a woman, too—but I loved her in a different, more refined way.

Most days, Tofu Roshi was a man to me, and I could not completely purify my feeling for him, no matter how hard I tried. I suffered at the hands of my own desire. I had hoped that after my jukai ceremony, Tofu Roshi would feel for me, the new Ichi Su, a deeper affection than he had felt for the old Susan, but to my great disappointment, he treated me exactly as before. I longed for his love, and I was ashamed of my longing.

Another year went by, and another, and another, and I decided to become a priest. This was a serious commitment, a commitment to devote my life to Zen practice, and to helping others along the way. But when I stepped back and looked at my life on the easel, I saw that I was already completely focused on Buddhism anyway. I didn't even go to the Next-to-Godliness Laundromat any more, because there was so much work to keep up with in the office. Tofu Roshi, who liked the laundromat much better than office work, took my laundry with him when he went. He sorted it by color and folded it neatly, but he lost even more socks than I did. His laundromat gatha went like this:

> With reptiles and insects, I shed my outer skin.
> I am one with everything that peels:
> Onions and bananas know how it feels.
> We all go together to the laundromat.
> Beside me at the big table,
> A grasshopper folds his freshly laundered shell.

In short, becoming a priest would not actually change the way I lived, but would only be a formal recognition, a public statement, of my commitment to the Buddha Way. I looked deep into myself to examine my motives, and I felt the time was right. Although there might have been a small part of me that wanted to take this step in order to win the high regard of Tofu Roshi, I didn't think it would be fair for that part to sabotage the interests of the part that wanted to become a priest for the right reasons.

There were two of us in the sangha who were ready to take this step. We would be the first priests to be ordained at No Way, and the first ever to be ordained by Tofu Roshi. The other was my dharma brother, a man with whom I had much karma—Shusansaki! We still shared the back apartment of the big house, and we continued to endure each other with difficulty.

Shusansaki was still Overseer of the Shoe Rack, and was still driven to distraction by disappearing shoes, usually new and expensive ones. I felt that in the interests of greater democracy and egalitarianism at the Zen Center, jobs should be rotated, and that it was time for somebody else to take over this responsibility. It seemed to me that Shusansaki was becoming too attached to his domain, and in general becoming rigidified in a law-and-order mentality. For example, he took out a subscription to a magazine called, "Tomorrow's Locks," and tried out all kinds of security measures. I don't think he got all his ideas out of the magazine—once he put a pre-set mousetrap inside every shoe after we'd gone into the zendo, and when we came out we stood around waiting while he sprang every trap with a stick so we could put our shoes back on. Another time he instituted what he called the "shoe-store display system." All visitors to the zendo were instructed to leave only one shoe on the shoe rack, and to bring the other one inside with them. Not a single shoe was stolen during the time we used this method, but the shoes got in the way in the zendo, especially during meals, when they stood like a fourth bowl next to the other three on the mealboard. After a nervous server ladled miso soup into Shusansaki's favorite flip-flop, the "shoe-store display system" was abandoned.

I didn't dare suggest the principle of job rotation because I was afraid that Shusansaki would want to become Tofu Roshi's secretary, and I would have to be Overseer of the Shoe Rack. But my job was different—it was separate from the daily functioning of the Zen Center itself, and it provided me with a means of support. I should explain that I worked well over forty hours a week, if you count the time I spent tying Roshi's shoes, in exchange for which I received room and board and a weekly stipend of five dollars, most of which I spent on socks. Other clothing I was able to get from our lost and found box, some of it quite attractive, though I hasten to say that I never took anything out of it which had been there less than ninety days. I know because Shusansaki dated every garment.

Now Shusansaki and I were equally beginners in the matter of learning to sew our priests' robes, and one evening a week we rode the BART train together to San Francisco, to take instruction from a very old Japanese man who was a friend of Tofu Roshi's. He had taken a vow of silence, and taught us wordlessly, by demonstration. Out of respect for his silence, we said our sewing mantra, "Unique New York," under our breath. Halfway through each sewing session we took a break, he clapped one of his hands together, and a young boy, probably his grandson, brought us Almond Sunset tea and Chinese fortune cookies. The old man always watched with delight as we drew our fortunes from the cookies, and then he opened his own and laughed out loud. I never knew what his fortune was, but I got the same one every week: "Don't let your heart lead you by the nose." On the way home one night, I asked Shusansaki about his fortune. He said he always got the same one, too, but his was different from mine. It was, "Don't wait for a dog to bring you your slippers." They were printed on little pink slips of paper, just like the fortunes you get in Chinese restaurants.

We finished our robes and were ordained as priests at last, in an intimate ceremony conducted by our beloved Tofu Roshi. This time I didn't invite any guests, because I was more confident in myself, and no longer needed to flaunt my Buddhism. Besides, Roshi held to the tradition of priests being required to shave their heads for their ordination ceremony, to show their commitment and humility, and it would have been hard on my mother to see me with my head shaved. Furthermore, watching me and Shusansaki standing together before a priest, she would have been constantly reminded of the wedding ceremony she wished me to be having instead, even if it was with Shusansaki. As a matter of fact, she had been rather partial to him ever since he had complimented her on a new pair of red shoes. "So few people notice footwear, anymore," she told me. "But Shusansaki knows that you can always tell a person by his shoes." When, several months later, the very same pair of red shoes disappeared from the shoe rack while Mom was inside the zendo at a special support group meeting for parents of Zen students, she didn't hold it against Shusansaki, but somehow seemed to feel that I was accountable. "The way you leave your shoes lying around, any riff-raff can run off with them," she complained.

"But, Mom, you're the one who left your shoes out."

"That's just what I mean," she said. "I didn't want to embarrass you, dear."

The first time my head was shaved, on the fresh and foggy morning of our ordination, Tofu Roshi himself did it, for me and Shusansaki both, with gentle, practiced hands. It's very difficult to shave your own head. A couple of weeks later, when a five o'clock shadow began to appear above my temples, I asked Tofu Roshi if he would help me again, and he agreed. First he shaved my head, and then I shaved his. Thus it became our custom to shave each other's heads. But he always reminded me that I didn't need to keep my head shaved if I wasn't comfortable with it, and that it was not the purpose of Buddhist practice to alienate one's parents. He explained that I must not become overly attached to the trappings of Buddhism, that a sincere and questioning attitude was more important than a smooth scalp. "How can you call no hair 'trappings'?" I asked. I felt that I still needed more time to overcome my self-consciousness and to declare myself a Buddhist with no holds barred. Additionally, I wanted to get beyond ideas of masculine and feminine. Just as Tofu Roshi's sex was unknown, so I thought that by shaving my head I might become a person of no particular gender.

To save time, Roshi and I fell into the habit of shaving each other's heads simultaneously. We faced each other, and he stood with his back to the mirror, so I could see the reflection of the back of his head. He couldn't see the back of my head either, of course, but he seemed to know it like the back of his hand. Here at last was a way for me to be physically close to my teacher within a spiritual framework.

One morning Roshi and I stood together thus in the office, our arms around each other in tonsorial care, the buzz of our two electric razors shutting out the rest of the world. Practicing mindfulness, I was completely attuned to the feel of Roshi's

"I had the sudden realization that I was shaving myself, that Tofu Roshi and I were one and the same."

skin beneath my fingers. Looking into the mirror, I had the sudden realization that I was shaving myself, that Tofu Roshi and I were one and the same. At that moment, the door opened and in walked Shusansaki. He stood as if frozen, clutching the morning mail. Roshi, whose back was to him, had neither seen nor heard him. Making a few last strokes at the nape of my neck he said, "I'm satisfied, Ichi Su. Are you?" I turned off my razor to speak to Shusansaki, though what I would have said I do not know, but he threw the mail on the floor, spun on his heel, and was gone.

Like a terrible earthquake, scandal shook our community. In its foaming wake, Roshi was asked to explain himself in an open meeting of the sangha. But the very morning of the meeting, I took a difficult step. I went away to stay in my friend Mercy's cabin in Mendocino County for a month, where there was neither electricity nor telephone, to let my hair grow, and to think through my relationship with Tofu Roshi and with Buddhism. I wanted to search into my own heart, uninfluenced by whatever the sangha might decide. I left a letter for Shusansaki on the kitchen table, in which I asked him to help Tofu Roshi with his correspondence while I was gone, and also to shave his head and tie his shoes. "And if you find out whether Roshi is a man or a woman, you are more intimate with him than I have ever been. My conscience is as clear as the driven snow. Your dharma sister, Ichi Su."

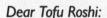

Dear Tofu Roshi:

Over a year ago, I started dating a really loving, emotionally mature man. We realized immediately that we were completely compatible, and we soon became serious about each other. We continue to be involved in a warm and deeply satisfying relationship. We have no problems. Help! What should I do? I have no past experience with this situation.

—Blown Away in L.A.

Dear Blown:

We always have a problem. If it's not one thing, it's another. This is our life: to work on our problems the best that we can.

I want to encourage you. You may be overlooking something. Does he ever forget to put the top back on the toothpaste tube? If the answer is no, and you can find no other difficulties, I suggest you plan to spend the holidays together, and have as house guests as many relatives on both sides as possible. Or take a long automobile trip together. This often turns something up.

I wish you luck. It would be a shame to have to break off such a beautiful relationship as yours for lack of a problem.

Dear Tofu Roshi:

There's this boy I really like at the zendo, and every time I sit next to him he peeks at me out of the corner of his eye. After zazen today, as we were brushing off our zabutons, I could swear he deliberately grazed my hand with his. Every time I hear the part in the sutra about "fulfillment of all relations," it sends shivers up and down my spine. Do you think I have a chance with him?

—Breathless

Dear Breathless:

Certainly you have a chance with him, but a chance for what? Perhaps it is a chance to bear and raise many healthy children together, and to live happily into old age together. Or perhaps it is a chance to experience disappointment. Only time will tell. In any case, do not fulfill your relations in the zendo itself.

Dear Tofu Roshi:

I joined my local Zen center because I want very much to meet a gentle man who has attained enlightenment. I figure that's the kind of guy for me. However, I've noticed that all the single fellows at the Zen center are incredibly anal retentive, if you'll excuse the jargon, and don't know how to express their feelings. I'm a real warm, expressive person who believes in letting the love I feel for others flow out of me. I was talking to a guy after zazen, and telling him about my breathing. When I gave him a little hug to say good-bye, he jumped back, and shouted something in Japanese or Sanskrit or some other language like that. Then he pointed to my shoes on the shoe rack and said, "Please don't use this shelf of the shoe rack. It's reserved for the priests." I thought that at a meditation center I would find some men who had learned to let their soft self out, but maybe I've picked the wrong tradition. Do you think I would have better luck in a vipassana or yoga center, for example?

—Yinny

Dear Yinny:

Cruising the meditation halls for a love partner is not the path to enlightenment. You must let go of your goal-seeking behavior if you wish to succeed. You must convince yourself that you are meditating in order to save all sentient beings. As for where to look, my observations are that vipassana meditation seems to attract many therapists, while poets and artists are drawn to the Tibetan practice. Cooks and carpenters like Zen, and yogic practice appeals to burnt-out academics. So keep these trends in mind as you look for a man who can express his feelings.

Dear Readers:

I wish to share the following letter with you, because it may be helpful to the many Buddhists who travel solo on the path to satori.

Dear Tofu Roshi:

I know that many folks nowadays are lonely and alienated, the nuclear family is falling apart and there's a high divorce rate even among spiritually-minded people. I would like to share with you and your readers what we did about this at our Buddhist center. We started a Study Group for Singles, which has met just once so far. The first meeting took place in the hot tub of one of our members, and the discussion topic was one of the aspects of the eightfold path: "having few desires." After the formal discussion was over we shared stories of "my most embarrassing moment in the zendo." The meeting was a big success, and next month we plan to focus on "Style and Design in Contemporary Buddhist Robes." It's going to be a potluck meeting, and everybody's going to bring a dish containing seaweed. At the third meeting we'll discuss the Third Grave Precept—not misusing sex—and follow up our discussion with a massage workshop. I hope your readers find some of these ideas helpful.

—Samadhi Single

Dear Tofu Roshi:

I fell in love with a Zen student, and we had a wonderful time. Not only did we study the sutras together, we engaged in all kinds of fun physical activities. But when the time came that we realized we had grown attached to each other, and that this attachment was a delusion, we knew what we had to do: we broke up.

Now I feel so calm and peaceful, knowing that I am putting an end to desire. Whenever I feel just a tiny bit sad about him, I know it means I need to practice harder. So I just want to say I believe in what you're doing, alleviating suffering and all with your advice column.

—Learned a Lesson

Dear Learned:

Thank you for sharing your experience. I hope it brings courage to other readers who are struggling to free themselves from the crippling delusion of earthly attachment.

Dear Tofu Roshi:

I'm deeply involved in Theravada meditation practice. I live with my boyfriend, who doesn't do any kind of meditation. He says watching sports on TV is his spiritual practice. My prob-

lem is that I find it hard not to be critical of him. When he isn't in front of the tube, he's reading The Sporting Green or muttering to himself about the NFL, and I just don't think he's developing his higher self. He's very accepting of my spiritual path, however, and is always encouraging me to go on over to the meditation hall. So if he's less judgmental than I am, maybe this means he is actually more spiritually advanced. Should I give up meditation for football? I've tried to persuade my boyfriend to come to our center and at least try meditation, but he says I'm offsides.

—Couch Potato's Girl

Dear Girl:

You are caught in dualistic thinking, in either/or mind. Ask your teacher to install a television in the meditation hall. Seat the home team fans on one side of the room and the visiting team fans on the other. You can chant the sutras during the commercial breaks. Your center should be responsive to the needs of the community. Additionally, you might be interested by the two letters that follow.

Dear Tofu Roshi:

My husband is a Buddhist, unfortunately. He has lately taken on a lot of responsibilities over at the meditation center, and

TOFU ROSHI

now it seems like he spends all his free time over there, sifting through ashes for stubs of incense, and cutting paper napkins in half. Or so he says. The dog hardly recognizes him anymore, and as for me, I bet he doesn't even remember whether my belly button is an inny or an outy. But when I suggest to Sam that he is neglecting important aspects of our family life, he looks at me like he can't believe how unenlightened I am. I'd like to know what's so significant about sifting ashes, anyway? I mean every single day? Couldn't you just leave a tiny little stub of incense in there for a day or two without completely ruining your chances of freeing yourself from the cycle of rebirth?

—Sam's Sarah

Dear Sarah:

There is nothing important about sifting ashes. That is why we do it. Try to convince your husband that there is nothing important about your family life either, and that there is nothing to attain by walking the dog or fulfilling the marriage vows. Tell him that if he walks the dog, it is emptiness in form, and if he makes love to you, it is form in emptiness. Hopefully, this will awaken his interest.

Dear Tofu Roshi:

This may be a long letter, but I just have to pour my heart out to someone. When my husband retired, my daughter-in-law—she's a lovely girl, but she's kind of a hippy, to tell the truth—she took him over by one of these Buddhist places, where everyone has shaved heads and you can't tell whether you're looking at a Mr. or a Mrs.—or Mizz, as my daughter-in-law would say. She thought he needed a new hobby. He's bald as a football himself, and about as pointy-headed, but without the lacing, so I guess he felt right at home there. I didn't know how lucky I was all those years he sat on his duff on a Barcalounger with his beer, after work. Now he gets up at 4:00 A.M. to drive across town and sit on a little black cushion, when he could be so much more comfortable at home. In order to get enough sleep, he has to go to bed at 8:00, or 8:30 at the latest.

The other night, my cousin and her hubby were coming into town on business, so we invited them for dinner. I worked all afternoon to make a lovely casserole, Parker House rolls, and a chocolate soufflé for dessert. Our guests were invited for 6:30, but the weather was real bad, we called the airport, and found out their plane was going to be late. At about 7:45, my Bert says to me, "Millie, these folks might not show up at all. I'll just get ready to turn in, now. That way I'll have a little more time to sit up with them if they do make it over."

At 8:00, the doorbell chimed. Our guests were full of apologies for being late, and they even brought us a nice wine to

TOFU ROSHI

go with dinner. Bert came to the table in his pajamas and robe, the one with the baseball logos all over it. "Bert, are you sick?" says my cousin Ginny.

"No," he tells her, "I just thought I'd save a little time by getting ready for bed early."

When I put the casserole on the table, Bert says, "Innumerable labors brought us this food." If that's his way of showing his appreciation for my cooking, I can do without it.

"Bert, honey, how can you say such a thing?" I exclaimed. I turned to Ginny and Jack. "It was really nothing," I told them. "It's just a simple meal."

When I went to put a helping on Bert's plate, he says, "None for me, dear, I've already brushed my teeth." There was an awkward silence, broken only by the clink of silverware and the snorty sound of Bert's breathing. Then Ginny and Jack began to tell us about their new deck, with a hot tub set into it.

"How often do you have to change the water?" I asked, just to keep the conversation going.

Just then Bert pushed back his chair, and made a funny little bow towards the Parker House rolls. "May we exist in muddy water with purity like a lotus," he said, and he went to bed. We didn't talk any more about the hot tub after that.

I don't remember what we did talk about, or how we got

through the rest of the evening, but, to make a long story short, Ginny and Jack left as soon as we'd all pushed the chocolate soufflé around on our plates some, and I cried the whole time I was putting the dishes in the dishwasher. Bert used to be such a thoughtful man, even if he was a little bit lazy. Why did Buddhism have to strike our home? Can you help me?

—Millie

Dear Millie:

I wish I'd been a guest at your dinner table! Your husband's zeal is misguided. A Buddhist eats what is put before him, especially if it has chocolate in it.

Time will almost certainly moderate your husband's piety, which tends to be extreme in the newly converted. In the meantime, in order to hasten your husband's return to the suchness of everyday life, don't cook him anything except boiled turnips, sit in his Barcalounger, and ignore him as much as possible. When he speaks to you, just press your palms together and bow slightly. He will soon see things as they are.

Dear Tofu Roshi:

I would like to talk to my husband, who passed on five years ago. Can you tell me how to do this? Will meditation help?

—Widow in Adrian, Michigan

Dear Widow:

Yes, I can tell you. This is not difficult. Prepare yourself by meditating alone in a room, after dark, by the light of a single candle. After about an hour, when you are in a calm and centered state, take three deep breaths, open your mouth (if it is not open already), and speak right up. Speak slowly and distinctly, and, if your husband was hard of hearing at the time of his death, loudly. But do not be afraid to speak with the passion of your soul. I think you will feel much better after you have talked to your husband, is it not so?

I cannot advise you on how to get him to answer you, but you do not mention this as a concern, in any case.

Dear Tofu Roshi:

My wife and I belong to a vipassana meditation group. Our community and our marriage have both been shaken by a new concept, ever since one of our most respected members brought a book to our center called Celibacy Within Marriage. *Our teacher, who is not married, and is unlikely ever to be asked, in my opinion, seems to think it's a very enlightened idea, and my wife is all for giving it a try, but I think it's just a crazy fad cooked up by some poor woman who didn't dare tell her husband he needed a bath. What really burns me up is that I grew up in a very strict Catholic family, and I was* probably the last man in America to remain a virgin until my wedding night. How could I have been so dumb? I told my wife I never would have "saved myself" for marriage if I'd known we were getting married for the purpose of legalizing our celibacy.

The reason I'm writing to you about this is that my wife says it's a matter of her spiritual development. She says she wants to try celibacy only because our sexual relationship has been so satisfying to her, but I think she's just trying to butter me up. I don't think a person can get any more out of celibacy than they put into it, and that isn't much. Excuse the question, Tofu Roshi, but are you celibate? If so, do you like it? I want to develop myself spiritually, too, and that's why I practice insight meditation. Is it really possible that "celibacy within marriage" could make me more potent spiritually? If so, I'd like to know just exactly how.

—Faithful Husband

Dear Husband:

One reason celibacy is not more popular is that it is viewed as a negative thing, simply as the absence of sexual activity. But with buddha mind we move away from such dualistic thinking. Celibacy is an activity in itself. At the deepest level, celibacy and sexual activity are one and the same, except that most people can be celibate more often, and keep it up for

"I have always been celibate with a number of different people at once."

longer each time they do it.

Your last question—how?—goes to the heart of the matter. There are many helpful how-to books about sex, but what we need now are some how-to books on celibacy, which avoid moralizing and outline the nuts and bolts of specific techniques and exercises for husband and wife, or lovers, to follow. But I leave the technology to the psychologists to develop.

As for celibacy within marriage, remember that like sex, celibacy is more meaningful when you do it with someone else. If you begin to feel rejected, remind yourself that your wife wants to be celibate with you.

Yes, I am celibate, and I get a great deal of pleasure out of it. But I could give it up any time, and so I would if I felt I was becoming too attached to it. I have never had the opportunity, as you do, to try celibacy within marriage. Rather, I have always been celibate with a number of different people at once.

I think you will find celibacy spiritually rewarding—a good way to explore the boundaries of the self, to keep awake to your life instead of getting stuck in unmindful habit. I would encourage you to try it for a day or two and then reevaluate it.

TOFU ROSHI

6. FAMILY LIFE - THE PATH OF THE HOUSEHOLDER

"Can a person stuck in full-lotus position fulfill his role as husband and father?"

With a heavy heart, wearing a new pair of Birkenstocks, I followed the sylvan path, all overhung with tresses of poison oak, to Mercy's cabin, for my month-long retreat from the backbiting, head-shaving world. I was confident no one would steal my sandals here. But my heart was heavy because I was worried about what might be taking place at No Way, and because I knew I had to take a long, hard look into myself, and examine yet again, at a deeper level, the nature of my attachment to my teacher, and even to Buddhism itself. The door of the little cabin stood open before me, and with one heartbeat following upon another, I stepped through the gateless gate. "Is there anybody here?" I called out to the emptiness.

"Yes, you old ricebag!" I answered myself. "Ichi Su is here."

"And who is this Ichi Su person, anyway?" I asked rudely, my feelings hurt at being called a ricebag.

"I guess you'll find out, if you really want to know," I said with a sigh.

In former times, in India, China, and Japan, it was generally necessary for the spiritual seeker to become a monk or nun in a monastery, or a hermit in a remote mountain retreat, in order to follow the path. Only a few wealthy emperors, who could afford to hire resident teachers for themselves, take long vacations, and not concern themselves with childcare, were able to cultivate wisdom without giving up the life of the householder. That women have been, through recorded history, so tied to home and family, is one of the many reasons we have been excluded from full participation in institutionalized religious practice. In Buddhist history, for example, we find only a handful of tales about nuns. But in America today, we are exploring the possibilities of what we call "lay practice." If Buddhism is to flourish, it must speak to people with jobs and families. And so in this chapter we include questions about integrating spiritual practice with ordinary life.

My own situation was unusual. Most people aren't able to give up their regular jobs, move into a Zen center and shave their heads. Nor are most people able to go on a solitary mountain retreat for a month. Paradoxically, it was while I was alone in the wilderness that I came to a new understanding of the significance of everyday life in the workaday world.

But my first concern was to sort out my feelings about Tofu Roshi, so that I could return to No Way with an understanding of what came next for me. I wanted to be completely open to the truth, whether it was that I should stay on as a priest at the

No Way Zen Center and offer to serve the sangha as Overseer of the Shoe Rack, or leave Zen practice altogether and go back to school to get a degree in counseling, as a normal young woman from my background would do.

I spent most of my time in meditation. At first I sat zazen; that is, "I" tried to follow "my" breathing, sitting in stillness with the question, "Who is it?" and "Who asks, 'Who is it?'" But a bad case of poison oak made stillness difficult if not impossible, and even when I pushed on to the question "Who asks, 'Who asks, "Who is it?"'" I could not get beyond the easy answer, "Ichi Su." And so I left off formal zazen to focus directly on my personal concerns. I thought about Tofu Roshi and me, about how it felt when he shaved my head, and how it felt when I tied his shoes. I waited for the truth. And when "it" itched, "I" scratched, and when "I" itched, "it" scratched.

The time of my retreat was early summer, and it soon became my habit to seek respite from the heat and itchiness in a playful stream that rested from its cartwheels in a quiet pool near the cabin, before it somersaulted on its merry way to the Eel River. I had the place all to my "self," at least as far as other human beings are concerned.

I had been on retreat for three weeks when some very bizarre events occurred, or seemed to occur. During all that time, I had not seen or spoken with anyone except Ichi Su (whoever *she* was). One midday as crackly as potato chips, after a long, hard morning of scratching meditation, I donned my robe, which I had brought with me because it was such a comfortable and versatile garment. I took a pretty blue bowl from the cabin in which to gather thimbleberries, and I sallied forth to visit my friend the stream.

There was a little beach beside my swimming hole, and just upstream from the beach, a knotted rope hung over the water, suspended from the overhanging limb of a cottonwood tree. I took off my robe, folded it neatly, and placed it on a big rock at the water's edge. My birthday suit doubled as a bathing suit. I had packed light for this retreat, but I had decided to bring along my birthday suit as well as my robe, because it was even more versatile, and almost as comfortable. I put the bowl on top of the robe to keep it from blowing away, and then I reached out over the water for the rope, climbed the mossy bank, sat on the knot and swung out over the stream. At the far extreme of the pendulum's swing, just over the deepest part of the pool, I heard myself give a great shout of "Whooizzit!" at the moment of letting go. The slack rope idled back toward shore, while I seemed to float like a cloud in perfect stillness above the water, my vaporous arms and legs stretching to the four winds. Then, feeling suddenly more like an apple than a cloud, I gave myself up to gravity, and my body, 98 percent water, joined with the water of the stream. Over and over again, like a little kid, I climbed the bank and jumped from the rope, by turns like a cloud, like an apple, like a fish, like a little kid again. "Who swings? Who leaps? Who falls? Who swims?"

I grew dizzy. When I bobbed to the surface of the stream for the umpteenth time, I saw a figure, a human figure, approaching the beach. It came to the water's edge. With a shock I recognized the tall, thin form of Shusansaki! "Greetings, dharma brother!" I called. Why had he come, and how had he found me? "Come on in—the water's fine." He made no answer. "Is anything wrong?" I shouted, but he didn't seem to hear me, didn't even look in my direction. "Hey, Shusansaki—It's me, Ichi Su. I forgive you. Will you forgive me?" But I could have been talking to the exact opposite of a sentient being for all the response I got. Well, perhaps he was pretending not to see me, so as not to embarrass me in my nakedness. I wouldn't put it past him, uptight as he was. "Hey, Shusansaki. Don't be embarrassed. I'm not completely naked, you know. I'm wearing my birthday suit."

I shouted in vain. Moving with deliberate calm, Shusansaki picked up my robe and bowl from the rock, and turned away. I noticed a couple of bandaids on the back of his head. He must have cut himself shaving. Then he turned the bowl upside down, put it on his head, and disappeared into the trees.

I hurried back up the hill to the cabin wearing nothing but my wet birthday suit and my sandals. My skin, still tingling with the freshness of the stream, now felt the touch of the dappled shadows of oak and madrone. Suddenly I knew that dressed exactly as I was, in leaf-shadowed skin and Birkenstocks, I was already wearing Buddha's robe—a field far beyond form and emptiness. All nature's creatures, all sentient beings, even if they are wearing nothing but their sandals, are dressed as priests. Shusansaki had taught me this lesson, by taking away my priest's robe, that was no robe at all. I hoped I'd catch up with him at the cabin, to thank him, and maybe get my non-robe back, but when I got there, I saw on the cabin porch not Shusansaki but a Mendocino County sheriff's deputy, making himself at home in the rocking chair. He showed me his badge and introduced himself as Benjamin Ross, "But everybody calls me 'Beany.'" He stared straight at me—my hair, after all, was still conspicuously short—while he explained he'd come to investigate a tip that marijuana was being cultivated on the property. "We got the call this morning in Ukiah—that's 'haiku' backwards." His staring made me uncomfortable, and I hastily put on a hat.

"If you're trying to figure out whether I'm a man or a woman," I said, "I wish you'd stop it. It's not an important distinction." I quoted my teacher, "If you've seen one sex you've seen them all." I assured him there was no marijuana being grown on the property, and reported the theft of my robe and bowl. Had he seen a tall, thin man with a shaved head? "I don't mean me," I added, in case my baldness had led him to the conclusion that *I* was a man.

He shook his head. "Tracking down a man in these hills is like trying to strike the moon with a stick," he said, but even so he asked me the details for the police report. When I came to the word "thimbleberry," he sighed with exasperation, tore off the sheet he'd been writing on, and handed me the pad and pen. "I can't spell well enough to graduate from dog school," he said, blushing. "Why don't you write it up yourself, so's to get the particulars just right." He was interested when I explained that the robe was a special Buddhist priest's robe that I had sewn myself. "Ain't that the darndest thing!" he exclaimed. "That means you could marry me or bury me, doesn't it? Wait till I tell the boys at the station I got a robbery call from a naked lady Buddhist priest."

We just sat and chatted a while. It was good to talk to another member of my species, and he didn't seem in any hurry himself. But he kept on staring, shifting his glance from one breast to the other like he was watching a tennis match. I explained that I didn't have anything else to put on, in between my hat and my shoes, and so he took off his shirt and gave it to me, after removing his badge and pinning it to a cute little undershirt he had on underneath. Thanks to his long shirttails, I was decently covered.

He was a friendly, low-key kind of a guy, even if he was a deputy. "I've got a lot of time to think," he said, "driving along these roads alone, and there's something I've been wondering about for a long time now. Maybe you know something about it, being a priest and all."

"What is it?" I said, encouraging him.

"That's it!" he exclaimed. "What *is* it? Do you know what I mean? What is *it*?"

He seemed pleased when I told him that Zen monks had been struggling with his question for centuries. "*I* can't wait to tell the folks back at the Zen Center that I met a sheriff's deputy in the woods who wanted to know what *it* is," I said. But I had to tell him the harsh truth, as I understood it—this was a question that nobody else could answer for him.

"I guess I kinda knew that," he assented.

"Well, Beany, can I offer you a cup of tea?" I asked, not wanting him to leave.

"Too hot for tea," he said, and took off his hat to fan himself. He was completely bald. "I guess I'd better be going. You can keep the shirt—just don't wear it around town, or I might get into trouble."

When he rose to go, I noticed that his shoes were untied, and told him so, checking the impulse to lean down and tie them for him.

"That's on purpose," he said. "My feet stay cooler this way. I'll keep my eyes peeled for your robe and your bowl, and you keep a sharp lookout for marijuana plants. I'll be back to check on you in a few days, and in the meantime, don't go marching around the woods in your birthday suit, especially with a robe thief on the loose. So long, priestess."

"Bye, Beany."

He shuffled up the hill to the road, his shoes flopping. I listened for the sound of his car starting, but I didn't hear it, so I walked up to the road myself, to see if he was having some kind of engine trouble. He was nowhere in sight.

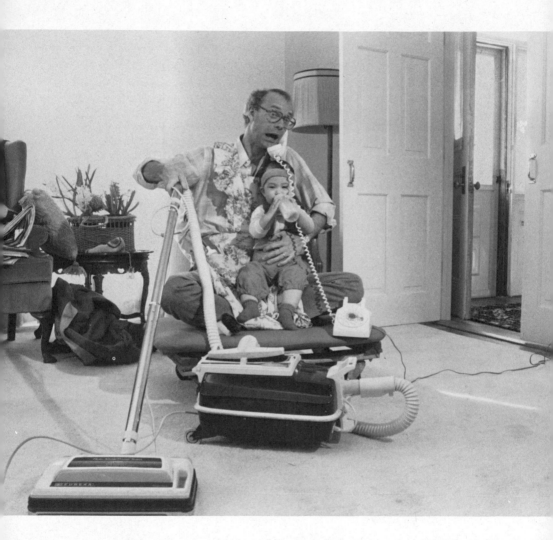

"Can a person stuck in full lotus position fulfill his role as husband and father?"

Dear Tofu Roshi:

My life is a mess. When I began meditating a few years ago, I had a lot of trouble with my knees. Sitting in lotus position was excruciating. But I persevered. I have a lot of will power and patience, when I have the time and the inclination. Finally I was able to sit in full lotus for twelve hours a day, painlessly, and then for twenty-four! Unfortunately, since that time I haven't been able to straighten out my legs. I've been going around on my knees and elbows for three months now. I wear my daughter's skateboard knee and elbow guards while she's at school and doesn't need them. But now she and my wife have started teasing me, and threatening to buy me a leash and collar. Also, it's difficult to prepare meals. What should I do? Do you think a person stuck in full-lotus position can still fulfill his role as husband and father?

—Lotus

Dear Lotus:

You could try preparing meals on a hibachi grill on the floor. I think you can be your daughter's father in any position, and as for being a good husband to your wife, make this an opportunity to explore new territory in the marital relationship.

Dear Tofu Roshi:

Please help me. I think Mom and Dad will be influenced by your opinion. I'm a thirteen-year-old girl with a problem. My folks are Vajrayana Buddhists, and until last year we lived in a big Buddhist commune. I learned to put my palms together and bow before I learned to walk or talk. The other kids and me used to sneak into the meditation hall and build playhouses out of the cushions. I used to think everything round was called a mandala—fried eggs, car tires, Mom's boobs. All us kids had names like Chakrasamvara and Hanuman. I liked mine best because it was the longest—Avalokiteshvara.

We recently had to move to a suburb of Cleveland, 'cause of Dad's job, and now I go to the local junior high. None of the kids in my class ever heard of a mantra, and nobody can say my name, not even my teacher. She says the human brain was not constructed to remember names of seven syllables. Now I want to change my name to Kitty, so I won't feel like such a weirdo, but my parents got all uptight about the idea. They say my heritage is nothing to be ashamed of. They always call me by my whole name, even though by the time they get finished saying it they usually forget what they were going to tell me to do, or else I did it already while they were saying my name, like cleaning up my room, for example. I asked Mom how she would have felt if her name was Avalokiteshvara instead of Bootsie when she went to Lake Forest High School. She said she probably would have wanted to change her name to Avalokiteshvara if she'd heard of it. She tried to change her name

TOFU ROSHI

to Iphigenia, which was the most exotic girl's name she knew of at the time, but everybody except her best friend kept right on calling her Bootsie. I shouldn't of even asked her, knowing what a weirdo she is. I guess she's satisfied now, though, 'cause before I was born Rinpoche gave her the name Ramalakirti. But Grandma and Grandpa still call her Bootsie.

Another problem is that I don't dare invite anybody over to my house because my parents are still working on their hundred thousand prostrations, and they usually are doing it right when I get home from school. I'd die of embarrassment if anybody saw. Even if we just went in the back door, you can still hear them, klunking down to the floor over and over, and the floor squeaks each time, and Dad's knees make a weird popping sound when he gets up. Klunk, squeak, pop, klunk, squeak, pop. I wish my parents would embarrass me in normal ways, like just making the bed creak when they're doing you know what. But they probably never do it, they have to spend all their free time bowing.

I don't want you to think I don't love my parents or anything like that, because I do, even if I give my Mom a hard time sometimes. For example, I used to love it when they let me polish the brass statue of Manjusri on the altar, and now I never want to do any of that stuff. "Why don't you want to do it anymore, Avalokiteshvara, honey?" Mom said. "I'm just not into it, that's all!" I said, and Mom started to cry. I guess they're too far out for me—I'm just not that type of person.

What should I do? Do you think I can get my parents to act more normal?

—Kitty

Dear Kitty:

You are in a difficult situation, but remember that your parents are struggling to keep their belief system alive in an alien environment, and this is probably why they overreact when even their own daughter no longer wants to support them in their religious practice.

I seriously doubt that there ever was a thirteen-year-old whose parents didn't embarrass him or her at one time or another. But I expect that most young people are embarrassed because their parents are so square and dull. Perhaps you can make an advantage of necessity. Just be direct. Say to a friend, "Want to come over after school and watch my parents do prostrations?"

You are now entering a difficult period in your relationship with your parents, but keep the lines of communication open, and when they are a few years older they will be able to accept you for who you are.

TOFU ROSHI

Dear Tofu Roshi:

I am the busy mother of two young children, and I also work part-time for my husband, an attorney, filing bankruptcy cases. Also, as you can imagine, our family life is full of neighborhood meetings, ballet lessons, house guests, building dioramas together, etc. Another thing is that our puppy broke his pelvis on a moving car, and I have to keep him from getting up and walking around. I don't have much time left over.

In the evenings after dinner, my hard-working husband relaxes by playing the banjo. I have tried to meditate while he is playing, but I can't seem to concentrate on my breathing during the "Foggy Mountain Breakdown." So the only time I can meditate is after he goes to bed. By the time I join him, feeling calm and centered, he's sound asleep. We haven't had time for even a simple conversation in months, and my marriage is falling apart. Should I give up meditation or give up my marriage?

—Abbie d'Armand

Dear Abbie:

Lose no time in going with your husband to a qualified Buddhist marriage counselor in your area, one who can help you to give up your dualistic thinking and find the way to integrate meditation practice into your married life. The path of the householder is a time-honored path. Because I have students who share your problem, I have, on their behalf, been investigating other ways of meditating besides sitting on a cushion for forty minutes at a stretch. We have begun to practice some of these methods at our Zen Center, and I offer you a few suggestions. When you are driving your daughter to her ballet lessons, and you come to a red light, put the car in neutral, put your foot on the brake, close your eyes and rest your fingertips lightly on the horizontal cross-piece of the steering wheel in the chauffeur mudra. Take five deep breaths and then open your eyes to see if the light has changed.

Your puppy's broken pelvis is an invitation from Samantabhadra, the shining practice bodhisattva, to curl up beside him—your puppy—on the kitchen floor, and breathe with him, meditating upon your oneness with all living beings.

Search for other ways to integrate your spiritual practice and your marriage. Chant the sutras while you build dioramas, and offer incense to the county clerk when you file a bankruptcy case. It is certainly neither my task nor my desire to separate husband and wife with the cutting edge of zazen.

Dear Tofu Roshi:

My brothers and I have had it. Mom is on a health-food kick, and she keeps trying to get us to eat tofu! She slips it into everything, thinking she'll pass it off as chicken. But we know that chickens don't have cubic breasts. So you are the only one we could think of who might know what we should do. We only eat regular food.

—Teddy

Dear Teddy:

This is not my field of expertise, but I must clear up an apparent misunderstanding on your part. Tofus don't have cubic breasts either.

In any case, my family name is not for food, but for a mountain in Japan where the wind in the trees whispers, "Tofu! Tofu! Tofu to you, too."

We eat what is put before us, no liking, no not-liking. If somebody puts a brussels sprout in your Hallowe'en bag, receive it gladly.

Dear Tofu Roshi:

We have a wonderful son, in college now. He's always been a good boy and had a paper route and everything. He was just home for a visit, and there was something changed about him. You could tell from the look in his eyes that his mind was maybe elsewhere, and I think I heard him speak to his soft-boiled egg before he cracked it. My husband said to me, "Mom, our boy's on drugs." So we read the pamphlet, "How to Tell If Your Child Is on Drugs." But it didn't say anything about the egg. Personally, I'm beginning to think he's meditating, I mean when we're not looking. How can you tell if your child is meditating? Sometimes he breathes loud.

—Mom in Occidental

Dear Mom:

Loud breathing, in combination with the incident with the egg, may indicate something. Count his breaths to see if he exhales and inhales the same number of times, as I recommend in my teaching. (If so, he may be one of my disciples!)

Here are some other things to look for:

Does he eat maddeningly slowly, chewing each bite as if to bring time to a complete standstill? Has he developed a peculiar, preoccupied walk, as if his feet are sticking to the floor? Does he bow to inanimate objects? Does he leave his shoes outside his bedroom door? Has he asked you to do likewise? Unlike the youth on drugs, the youth who meditates is likely to suggest to his parents that they make certain changes in their "life style," such as sitting on the floor or eating with chopsticks, or even doing both at the same time.

Watch for the physical paraphernalia that show up in the home of a meditator. Incense, of course, is one. As are flowers on top of the toilet, and round, firm cushions about sixteen inches in diameter.

Furthermore, different symptoms may indicate different

T O F U   R O S H I

kinds of meditative practice. The sufferer who repeatedly lies down on the floor on his stomach and then gets up again is probably on the Tibetan path. The one who takes up hugging of parents and prolonged wordless eye contact may be doing some kind of Christian contemplation, or perhaps nothing more addictive than group therapy. If your child manifests a new obsession with symmetry, folding his paper napkin neatly and lining things up at right angles or parallel to each other— silverware, pencils, toothpicks—he is probably practicing Zen meditation.

I can't tell from your letter whether you have cause for concern. You might seek help from your local support group for parents of meditators. Additionally, you may send for my booklet, "How to Tell If Your Teenager Is Meditating," which expands upon the comments I have just made.

Dear Tofu Roshi:

If everything we do is part of our practice, why do I have to practice the piano?

—Laura Jean

Dear Laura Jean:

We all need form and discipline to develop ourselves. It is said that even Bodhidharma, when he was a young monk, practiced scales for an hour a day. And did you know that he cut off his eyelids so that he would not fall asleep at the keyboard? Later, when you are more fully realized, you will be able to practice the piano simply by raking the pebbles in the courtyard of the compound, weaving watertight baskets out of rushes, or playing games of video.

Dear Tofu Roshi:

My teenage daughter has taken up some kind of Eastern meditation, and as part of her new way of life she's become a strict vegetarian. This would be all right with me, except that she wants to impose it on every living thing around her, including our cat. The other day she came into the kitchen as I was giving Cataract his dinner of kibbles. She screamed and threw up her hands and said, "Oh, that's so brutal, how can you give him those poor dead kibbles to eat? Do you realize how they kill them?" I read the package and they do have animal products in them, but I don't think a kibble is a kind of animal, is it? My daughter seized the cat's dish from my hand and bowed as she gently emptied it into the lock-top garbage bin. Then she arranged an attractive serving of cold asparagus salad with walnut oil dressing on Cataract's dish, but I don't need to tell you whether the cat ate it or not.

You know how passionate teenagers are, when they take on a cause. My daughter is a sweet girl, but she's getting carried away. Every time she finds a food item in our house that contains dead animal products, she bows and chants to it. Yesterday she conducted a memorial service for half a gallon of butter pecan ice cream, because it turns out it contains cow hooves. She spends hours preparing nouvelle cuisine vegetables for Cataract, in a vain attempt to arouse his appetite. I'm afraid he's going to starve to death. I believe there is an organization called "Buddhists Concerned for Animals." Do you know of them, and do you think they could persuade my daughter to let the cat have his kibbles?

—Cat Lover

Dear Cat Lover:

It is a credit to you that you have raised a child who exerts meticulous effort to save all creatures of the animal kingdom. If we all had the wholeheartedness of adolescents, this would be a better world. But even as we vow to save all sentient beings, we must live with the terrible possibility that we will step on a kibble and fall short of our goal. The organization you want is not Buddhists Concerned for Animals, but Animals Concerned for Buddhists. They would probably send over a few appreciative cows and pigs to take your daughter out for the evening and tell her to relax and enjoy herself, that it is not incumbent upon her to have a funeral service for every single kibble that's passed to the other shore.

Dear Tofu Roshi:

What is your opinion about so-called "women's spirituality"? I have learned to be a feminist from my wife. She has helped me to realize and express the feminine side of my nature, the intuitive side, the part that likes to do a little flower-arranging, or daydream over an extra cup of decaf in the morning, while she helps the kids practice their soccer skills in the back yard. For my part, I've encouraged her to assert herself, to express her anger by standing up to our landlord, to develop her math skills by balancing our checkbook and doing our tax forms, and I've put her in charge of home maintenance and car repair. Sometimes I even let her win at chess, in order to give her confidence in her left-brain thinking, while I am exercising my nurturing, self-effacing side.

Anyway, my problem is that she is about to go to a "women's spirituality retreat," at a resort with hot springs, saunas, masseuses, and all those women walking around naked. I don't want to be left behind with the kids. That this retreat should be for biological women only seems to contradict my wife's assertion that there is a feminine part of me. If she was a true feminist, I think she'd let me go in her place, to develop my anima, and she'd stay home and change the oil in the car, which should have been done a long time ago, anyway. Isn't she being inconsistent? We are all one.

—Hermaphrodite

TOFU ROSHI

Dear Herm:

Someday you will be ready for women's spirituality. But from your letter I sense that you need to prepare yourself first, through practices of a more ascetic kind, such as sleeping on a bed of nails and wearing a hair shirt, but not at the same time.

Let your wife go on this retreat, and take advantage of her absence to develop your anima right at home, by doing some extra mending, ironing, and carpooling for the kids. Surprise your wife by waxing the kitchen floor while she's away, and have an apple pie cooling on the window sill to welcome her home.

Dear Tofu Roshi:

My wife and I have practiced Tibetan Buddhism since before our only daughter was born, and our bells and chants and meditations have been a familiar part of her growing up. But now that she's reached adolescence, she's begun openly rejecting our way of life. As you can imagine, it deeply saddens us to see her rebelling against the values we have tried to instill in her, and we don't know what to do.

Our daughter is named after Avalokiteshvara, the bodhisattva of compassion, but lately she's started complaining about her name. And here's another thing—one of her household jobs has always been to polish the little brass figure of Avalokiteshvara that we keep on our altar. But last week our

Avalokiteshvara flatly refused to polish the brass Avalokitesh-
vara, and the next day we noticed with a shock that the figure
of Avksh. (Forgive the abbreviation, but I can't be bothered to
write the whole thing out every time) had been replaced on
the altar by a little orange plastic figure of Garfield, the cat.
We found Avksh. in the bathroom cabinet between the un-
flavored and the mint dental floss, and we switched Avksh. and
Garfield around again, without saying anything to our daughter
about it, because we were at a complete loss for what to say.

What happened yesterday afternoon was even more upset-
ting. My wife and I both took off from work early and retired
to our bedroom to spend some longed-for time together on our
hundred thousand prostrations. As we bowed our way through
a peaceful afternoon, I thought I heard muffled laughter, but I
was so thoroughly engrossed in my practice that I paid no
attention. We stopped, as we usually do, after five hundred
deeply satisfying bows, and I reached under the bed to get
my slippers. And what do you suppose I saw? There was our
daughter, lying on her stomach under the bed, flanked on
either side by a schoolmate! On being discovered in their hid-
ing place, all three of them burst into hysterical giggles.

"Avksh!" I said in as firm a voice as I could muster. "You
come out from under there this instant and apologize. Look
what you're doing to your poor mother!" My wife, Ramalakirti,

T O F U   R O S H I

was sitting in a heap on the floor, sobbing. I tried to comfort her: "Don't cry, Ramalakirti, honey. Avksh. will say she's sorry, won't you, Avksh.?"

The giggling changed to sniffling, and a sullen reply came from under the bed. "I've changed my name to Garfield."

She stayed under the bed, but her two friends crawled out, blushing with embarrassment. "I'm sorry, Mr. Gilligan," said one.

"Gosh, Mrs. Gilligan," said the other, "that was really a gas, the way you were bowing and everything. It was very educational."

"We have to go home, now," said the first. "But thanks a lot for the nice time."

Then we all left the room except for Avksh., who didn't come out from under the bed for hours.

Where did we go wrong?

—Avksh.'s Dad

Dear Avksh.'s Dad:

Your daughter is going through a stage. I feel sure she loves you and your wife, Rmkrt., very deeply. I think you should be more flexible with her. Go ahead and call her Garfield, if that's what she wants. What's the harm in that? Or call her

Kitty, which is a real name, and an appropriate nickname for Avalokiteshvara.

You could even put the little Garfield figure back on the altar, and have her polish it, instead of polishing You Know Who. Put Y.K.W. back in the bathroom cabinet. Between the unflavored and the mint dental floss is an honorable place for the bodhisattva of compassion.

7. PHILOSOPHICAL CONCERNS

"Why is there something, rather than nothing?"

I walked through the gate of the No Way Zen Center, dressed in Beany Ross's deputy's shirt and a skirt I'd stitched together out of California buckeye leaves and paper towels from the cabin. I'd made it for the Greyhound bus trip down to Oakland, so people wouldn't stare at me, and I'd repeated my sewing mantra with every stitch.

"Is anybody here?" I called out, but there was no answer. Nobody was home, not even an old ricebag. So I walked right over to the Next-to-Godliness Laundromat, in hopes of finding Tofu Roshi. I was eager to tell him what I had realized in the wilderness of Mendocino County.

Pausing to look through the window, I was arrested by my own reflection in the glass. I hadn't looked in a mirror since I'd left. I did look a little strange. My hair had grown to crew-cut length, but what really shocked me was that something else had grown as well—my earlobes! As I studied my face in the laundromat window, it seemed to go fuzzy, like a newspaper photograph out of registration, and then it divided into two faces, like a double exposure, and the two faces moved apart from each other and came into focus separately, and one of them was my reflection, and the other was no reflection, but the familiar face of Tofu Roshi, flanked on either side by a dangling earlobe! His hair was growing out, too. Our eyes met, and he raised a forefinger to beckon me in. Inside, we bowed to each other, and he stepped back to regard me. "I like your outfit," he said, "but it could use a wash. Do you wish me to pop it in with my things?"

I shook my head. "No thanks. I've nothing else to put on at the moment. But tell me, Roshi, are we one or are we two?"

"Not two!" he shouted, so loud that it caused a couple of heads to turn in the laundromat.

"But Roshi, who is the teacher and who is the student?"

"Do not be dualistic," he said with a tired smile. "Teacher or student, man or woman . . . I am sick of it! My large news is that I'm the new manager here! Believe me, Ichi Su, everyday life is where *it* is *at*."

In this final chapter we deal with questions of a general philosophical nature, questions about form and emptiness and the meaning of life, questions about enlightenment and its relation to lightbulbs. Almost everyone whose spirit reaches for the truth like a young sapling reaching for its mother's breast has at one point asked herself or himself, "Who are you, again? I didn't catch your name the first time."

When I went on retreat, I took with me many philosophical questions, such as: Who am I? Who is Tofu Roshi? Do I love him in the wrong way? What's it all about, anyway?

I came back from my retreat with a renewed spirit, a sincere desire to struggle for the enlightenment of all sentient beings, even the most ordinary ones. I knew now I didn't need Tofu Roshi in order to continue my practice, that my own life could be my teacher: the rope swing, the poison oak, the Greyhound bus. I learned that an ordinary man like Beany Ross could ask the same profound questions as a Zen master, and that I could learn from the Beany Rosses as well as the Tofu Roshis. And vice versa. I learned, when Shusansaki disappeared into the woods with my robe, not to be attached to particular forms— that a priest's robe might as well be made of leaves and paper towels. I was ready for anything.

I found out from my dear friend Mercy what had happened while I was gone. At the meeting on the very night of my departure, Tofu Roshi had been asked by the sangha to explain his apparently improprietous behavior with me. "Shaving is just shaving," he said. "Nothing special." But there remained some, among them Shusansaki, who felt that what had been improprietous was that Tofu Roshi and I were shaving each other's heads at the same time. Someone had demanded, "Roshi, tell us whether you're a man or a woman, so we know how to interpret your actions." But Tofu Roshi wouldn't tell. He said it was a matter of no importance.

After a lengthy meeting, all had finally agreed that Tofu Roshi should take a leave of absence from the No Way Zen Center, let his hair grow, and return in a month's time, when everybody could take a fresh look at the situation. The sangha also felt it was appropriate that I had taken a self-imposed leave of absence, although I was not held accountable to the same degree as Tofu Roshi, I being the student.

Tofu Roshi took a room in a rooming house and began to spend all his time at the Next-to-Godliness Laundromat. "But what about the compost heap?" I asked Mercy. "We all took turns," she said. Shusansaki kept up with the essential office work during the month, except for the letters to the advice column, which he saved for me. Mercy and her little daughter moved into my old room, in the back apartment with Shusansaki. "He's really changing, Ichi Su," she said. "He's not as monk-like as he used to be." Apparently he went away for a couple of days to some kind of men's retreat up in Mendocino County, "not far from my cabin," and returned a softer, humbler person, who no longer insisted on rigid adherence to form. He even stopped shaving his head and wearing his priest's robe, saying he didn't wish to set himself apart by wearing something special, although sometimes he walked around with a bowl on his head, to cover his still-bare scalp. She said they had carefully packed up my belongings in boxes, and she was

TOFU ROSHI

keeping them safely for me till I decided what I was going to do next. "You can have your room back if you want it," she assured me. "We'll figure something out. The baby and I could even stay in Shusansaki's room, temporarily. You may not believe this, Ichi Su, but I think we're in love. He's really different. He's not putting out those paranoid vibes anymore, and I think that's why not a single pair of shoes has disappeared from the shoe rack for the longest time—weeks and weeks."

As it happened, Tofu Roshi's month-long probation was up and the community meeting was scheduled for the very night of my return. The meeting was held in the zendo, the only room large enough to hold us all. Tofu Roshi ambled up the walk to the shoe rack as I was taking off my flip-flops. Because it was a big meeting, the shoe rack was already crowded. "You may put them on the bottom shelf," he told me, indicating the special spot reserved for the head priest's shoes. "I do not mind."

We went into the zendo and settled down, as more and more people came in behind us, found cushions, and fitted themselves into the gaps on the floor like pieces of a jigsaw puzzle. Shusansaki, incredibly, was late. I imagined him lingering outside to straighten up the piles of shoes on the shoe rack. I was a little nervous about seeing him—I hadn't seen him since he took away my robe and bowl, and the time before that was when he walked in on me and Roshi shaving each other. Outside the zendo, cats howled. It was a chilly evening, and I noticed Roshi shivering, so I took off my deputy's shirt (I had another shirt on underneath) and passed it to him. He put it on with obvious delight, straightening his shoulders and pointing with a grin to the embroidered emblem that said "Beany Ross, Deputy Sheriff, Mendocino County."

When Shusansaki came in at last, our eyes met and we bowed to each other. I silently mouthed the question, "Where's my robe and bowl?" He pointed to the altar, and there was a bowl, the very same chipped blue bowl from Mercy's cabin, containing an offering of fuzzy kiwi fruit, that looked like little monks' heads with the hair just starting to grow out. He shrugged as if to ask, "Is that it?" and I nodded. "Robe?" I mouthed again. He shook his head and put a finger to his lips.

Mercy was running the meeting, and she began by reading the agenda:

Roshi's role at No Way
    Is he a man or a woman?
    Do we want him back in either case?
    How can we all take responsibility for preventing abuses
        of the teacher/student relationship?
What about Ichi Su?
    What's happening with the letters column?

Updates
    shoe rack
    compost heap

With such an agenda as this, touching on all the essential points of our practice, we settled in for a long meeting under Mercy's patient guidance. But the meeting was over almost before it began.

Tofu Roshi announced at the outset that he was grateful to the sangha for requesting that he take a leave of absence, because otherwise he might never have become manager of the Next-to-Godliness Laundromat. "This is where my path lies now," he said. "I've come to realize that I can better serve my fellow beings as a laundromat manager than as your head priest." He said that if leadership was what the sangha wanted, he was confident that Shusansaki and I could provide it, that it was not his wish to abandon us, and that he would be glad to return to the Zen Center from time to time as a visiting lecturer. If anyone wished to have an interview with him, it would be his pleasure to hold dokusan in his little office at the back of the laundromat, while the clothes were in the dryer. "Let us continue to practice together," he said. "You shall be my teacher, I shall be yours, and everyday life will teach us all."

"What about the compost heap?" asked Shusansaki.

"I have lost interest in it," said Roshi. "It gets the clothes so dirty. Cannot you take it on, Shusansaki? I think it would be good for you—it would loosen up your thinking."

"But who will look after the shoe rack, while I'm shoveling compost?"

"Let the shoe rack look after itself," said Roshi. "Is it not true that shoes have stopped disappearing?" And Shusansaki, with his newfound adaptability, agreed.

"What about the letters column?" Mercy asked.

"Let Ichi Su keep it going," he said. "She knows what I would say better than I do myself. She always has. I am no longer Tofu Roshi. Let her be Tofu Roshi. I think I will change my name to Beany, as it says here on my shirt."

It seemed that everything was settled. I was invited to move into Tofu Roshi's old apartment, and to continue the office work and particularly the letters column, on the condition that I neither shave my head nor wear a robe. "We're trying to get away from everything that separates people," Mercy explained. I was happy to be able to report my own change of heart on these very matters. I said my skirt of leaves and paper towels was a good enough robe for me. "It's a far-out skirt," said Mercy. "What kind of leaves is it made of?"

"Leaves of absence," I explained. I was grateful for the sangha's forgiving attitude, although I knew I'd done nothing wrong. How lucky I was to be practicing with a supportive community of people who were united by a shared desire to see things as they are, and to see nothing as it isn't!

Tofu Roshi that was, now Beany the second (but he'll always be Tofu Roshi to me), was eager to get back to the laundromat, and our meeting came to an end. As we rose from our cushions, a voice called out from the back of the zendo, "Tofu Roshi, tell us, finally, are you a man or a woman?"

I looked at Roshi and he looked back at me and shrugged. I suddenly felt called upon to speak. "There is no Tofu Roshi but ourselves," I replied, with a new confidence. "I am Tofu Roshi, you are Tofu Roshi. Male or female, soft curd or hard curd, we are all teachers, we are all students, we are all Tofu Roshi."

I slept that night in Tofu Roshi's bed, and the next day I unpacked my few things and put them away in my new quarters. When I opened the closet, I got quite a shock. Hanging on the inside of the closet door was one of those cloth shoe keepers, with a pair of shoes in every one of its many pockets— aerobics shoes, basketball shoes, Italian sandals, Clark's Wallabies, and even the new Birkenstocks I'd lost that first day during zazen instruction! And neatly tucked into every pocket between the shoes was a rolled up pair of clean socks. As it turned out, we were eventually able to return almost all the shoes to their rightful owners (including Tofu Roshi himself), and those that remained were sold in our annual flea market.

The socks were all mine, and now I just keep them there like kangaroo babies in their little pouches. I won't have to buy any more socks for a long time.

I have come to the conclusion that Tofu Roshi was acting under an uncontrollable impulse to find a pair of shoes he'd be able to tie by himself; that he was only borrowing the shoes until such time as he learned to tie a bow. Nobody is perfect, not even a Zen master. I don't know about the socks. But much is beyond our understanding and we must learn to live with this truth. As for my robe, Shusansaki was vague about it. When I went to Mercy's cabin the following spring, for a peaceful weekend alone, there was my robe, hanging on a nail inside the door, with a spider dangling from its sleeve. I left it in the cabin for subsequent visitors to use as a beach robe.

Tofu Roshi is still our teacher. He gave a lecture in the zendo just the other day, entitled, "Getting the grease stains out of your buddha nature." He recommended certain soap products, and went on to say that "Life is like a washing machine—it is a transforming process. And like a washing machine, you do *not* always get out of it what you put into it. Contrary to popular opinion. There are always going to be some surprises."

I still work in the office every day, answering the letters that come pouring in, addressed to "Dear Tofu Roshi." And I feel that I answer for him, that he speaks through me. This morning when I looked in the mirror to put on some earrings, I changed my mind and decided not to wear any. I guess I've been wearing such heavy earrings lately that they've stretched my earlobes out, so now they look all long and dangly.

Dear Tofu Roshi:

How many Zen masters does it take to change a light bulb?

—Plum Blossom

Dear Plum Blossom:

Two. One to change it and one not to change it.

Dear Tofu Roshi:

Will we ever get to see a picture of you? My wife says maybe you don't exist. If you do exist are you a man or a woman, and how old are you if you're a man? I enclose a snap of I and my wife at our silver anniversary.

We like your column even if you don't exist. Thanks.

—Frank

Dear Frank:

Here is a hint about my appearance: Do you know what bean curd looks like?

As to your wife's concern—do I exist at all?—I answer with an American folk expression: Does a bear sit in the woods?

Dear Tofu Roshi:

I made a bet with my wife that you don't print real letters, you just make them up. No real person would write in with those wacko questions. If you print this letter I have to change

all the burnt-out light bulbs in our house for the next month,
unless I can convince my wife that you made up this letter, too.
                                        —Still in the Dark

Dear Still:
   The letters are real. It is I, Tofu Roshi, who am not.

Dear Tofu Roshi:
   What I want to know about enlightenment is, can you read
by it?
                                        —Perry Mitty

Dear Perry:
   First, be sure you have fresh light bulbs.
   Second, consider the koan called "The Sound of One Hand
Scratching." No Bun once asked Bush Wak, "If a mosquito
bites Buddha, will it become enlightened?"
   Bush Wak frowned and scratched his left ankle.
   Suddenly No Bun slapped his forehead.
   Commentary by Za Phu: Thus No Bun attained enlighten-
ment and killed a mosquito at the same time.

Dear Tofu Roshi:
   Why is there something, rather than nothing?
                                        —Auntie Matter

Dear Auntie:

You have probably heard the wise old saying: "Time is nature's way of keeping everything from happening at once." Similarly, something manifests in order to keep nothing from taking up all the space.

In this matter which you present, nothing could be more material to our understanding of what is than what is not. We must learn to see things as they are and to see nothing as it isn't. In substance, nothing matters.

Dear Tofu Roshi:

Why are all you gurus and swamis and roshis, etc., men? When will you get with ERA?

—Berkeley Sister

Dear Sister:

I am interested to learn that there are nuns in Berkeley. As a member of a holy order, you wish to know why we religious leaders are not gods, incarnate, but mere mortals, mere men. We are still but men because we are not yet beyond the Wheel of Karma. But do not ask us to be with the era, for though we live in the present era, our souls are not of this era, and we aspire to break out of its temporal bonds.

T O F U   R O S H I

Dear Tofu Roshi:

  What is the meaning of life?

  —Samadhi Pantz

Dear Readers:

  I am almost certain we studied this controversial subject in the monastery where I trained, but it was long ago, and by the time I received the above letter, I was unable to recall the answer. Therefore, I called for assistance from the readers of my column, and I here share with you some of the letters from those who took time out from their busy search for the meaning of life to respond to my query.

Dear Tofu Roshi:

  I feel sorry for that poor sucker who wrote in asking about the meaning of life. MEANING?!?!?! . . . LIFE?!?!?! . . . Poor sucker.

  —No Dummy

Dear Tofu Roshi:

  This is the first time I ever wrote in to an advice column, but I just had to speak up about the meaning of life. Lots of people will tell you that there's no meaning in life, you should just have fun while you can. People will try and persuade you to have sex with them on that basis. That's why I'm writing *in, because I know a lot of people are obsessed with the idea that the only meaning there is, is just in screwing around. But there's more to life than sex, believe me. Don't let anyone tell you the only real pleasure is pleasure of the flesh, or the only enlightenment is the oneness of sexual union. I bet a lot of letters come in to you about the peak experiences resulting from tantric practice and Dionysian rites, and other types of orgies. We should ignore these lewd voices. Some people just can't think about anything except sex, whether it's remember-ing pleasurable moments of the past, or fantasizing about what they would like to do, or who they want to have do what to them, in which position, or on what piece of furniture, and all that. So I just wanted to inject a less salacious note into the debate on the meaning of life, and to say that the first step toward understanding the meaning of life is to get your mind out of the gutter. Don't think about sex.*

—Chaste Thinker

Aedr Fotu Sorhi:

Life: a ootl usually of rahdened etsel tiwh tucting dirges rof rofming or omsothing rusfaces, pse. of temal.

Niscerely,
—Bewster S. Vesenth

TOFU ROSHI

Dear Tofu Roshi:

I shave my head in order to maintain an attitude of humility, but the loss of body heat through my seventh chakra is causing my health to deteriorate. I find there is a close connection between a cold head and a head cold. Last week I surrendered to desire and began to wear a head covering in the zendo. Now my head is warm, but somewhere inside of it my con-science is bothering me. I am caught between the Scylla and Charybdis of guilt and physical discomfort, respectively.

—Balmoral Snood

Dear Balmoral:

You should have your head examined. The guilt you are experiencing is purely psychological. Cover your pate with whatever headdress is consonant with the traditional attire of your practice, and say to yourself, "My conscience is clear as a bell." Avoid heavy headwear, as it puts undue strain on the neck muscles.

Dear Tofu Roshi:

I'm trying to save all sentient beings. I thought it would be easier to start with the small ones, so I need to know if this includes bacteria.

—A Sincere Student

"My conscience is clear as a bell."

Dear Sincere:

   A moot point. Start with something that is at least visible to the naked eye, like a housefly. It is difficult to tell when a staphylococcus, even a large one, is in proper zazen posture.

Dear Tofu Roshi:

   I have been a faithful reader of your column for over two years, but I never thought I would write you. I was wrong, wasn't I?

—Deluded

Dear Tofu Roshi:

   I understand that a basic part of your teaching is to forget the self. But I am a psychotherapist, and the self is the very thing that I work with. Sigh by sigh, tear by tear, fist by fist, and dream by dream, my clients rebuild their sense of self; and then you come creeping up behind them and—WHACK!— you hit 'em on the back with a stick, and the fragile structure topples to the ground in a heap. In five heaps, I am told. How do you reconcile this apparent contradiction between spiritual development and psychological health? Do you think we are working against each other?

—Jane

Dear Jane:

You are right—we cannot forget the self until we have a strong self to forget. The work you do, therefore, prepares a person for the work I do, and for this I am grateful to you, wherever you are. You knead the dough, I bake it in the oven of the zendo. That is why, at our practice place, every new member must have a certificate of mental health before being allowed to join. But even this is not always sufficient.

For example, one of our members, who forgot the self during a long sesshin, was completely unable to recall it (the self) when the sesshin was over. Luckily, we knew his name and address, and were able to send him home in a taxi. He remained confused for some months, believing Bodhidharma to be the president of the United States. Another student had a deep experience of no-self, or anatta, during retreat, and when, at the end, she returned to the self, it was the self all right, but it was the self of someone else. When she asked herself in the final moments, "Who am I?" and, "Who asks, 'Who am I?'" she apparently noticed the name of Dan Flanagan, embroidered on the zabuton on which she sat. She unsuccessfully tried to enter his bag of skin, his house, his truck. But he, of course, was already there, and there was not sufficient room for both of them, at least not in the bag of skin. Nor did he particularly want her in his house or truck. Only through the

TOFU ROSHI

concentrated effort of further zazen was she able to forget Dan Flanagan's self and subsequently to reenter her own.

Since that time, we require everyone to wear tags around their necks in the zendo, with their name, address, occupation, pet peeve, and the name of the president of the United States. (In some cases the last two items are the same.) Thus, our students can transcend the self during meditation, in confidence that the answer to the questions "Who asks, 'Who am I?'" and "Who asks, 'Who asks, "Who am I?"'" is within easy reach.

Dear Tofu Roshi:

In my past lives, I was a lactobacillus, a ladybug, a laboratory rat, a saddle horse, and a dental hygienist, in that order. As you see, there is a theme of service that runs through all of my former lives, and explains my rapid climb up the karmic ladder. Sometimes I've been male, and sometimes female, except, of course, when I was a lactobacillus. I was a male ladybug, by the way, and enjoyed the transvestite lifestyle. Now I am a brain surgeon, rich and famous, but unfulfilled. It turns out that status isn't my thing.

I recently heard about an ancient method according to which it is possible to consciously direct future rebirth. Can I go back to being a ladybug? That was the happiest time of my lives. My mouth still waters when I see aphids.

—Dr. Medulla

Dear Dr. Medulla:

Yes, there is such a method. In Soto Zen we do not speak much about these things, because too much deliberation about the choice of a future life can make us lose our focus on the life we are living. Furthermore, the training in this method is very difficult, the competition for future lives is intense, the whole process is even worse than applying for college, and many people are not reborn into their first-choice lives. How would you feel about being an earwig, for example? If this would be acceptable to you, contact your local Center of Conscious Rebirth.

APPENDIX

HOW TO GIVE UP SELF-IMPROVEMENT

I want to talk to you today about the importance of giving up self-improvement. This is one of our hardest tasks, as we train ourselves to follow the Buddha Way. In this modern age, we are met at every turn by new and tempting opportunities to improve ourselves. We are offered everything from workshops on how to be a better parent to classes in strengthening the quadriceps. We are so deeply habituated to this way of thinking that we do not even recognize it in ourselves. This is the great danger. How many of you first began to sit zazen with the hope that it would in some way make you a better person? For many of us it may take years of hard practice before we are completely sure that we have hoped in vain. Buddhism teaches us that everything always changes, but we must finally admit that it does not change for the better.

When old Bush Wak was still master at the monastery on Lazy Man Mountain, a young monk with flabby thighs said to him, "My mind dwells always on the five desires (food, sex, sleep, fame, wealth). Last night I ate all the lychee nuts in the monastery storeroom. How can I conquer my weaknesses and become a better person?"

"You ricebag, you!" snarled Bush Wak. "Who wants to be a good person? Lie down without delay and take a nap till the feeling passes. How can you be awakened if you are not asleep?"

Za Phu has given us this verse:

The old ricebag and the young ricebag grumble on Lazy Man
Mountain.
How they annoy each other with their unpleasant personalities!
The young ricebag falls asleep.
When he awakes he will still be a sickly ricebag.

"But what's so bad about self-improvement?" you may ask. Perhaps you have disagreeable character traits or weak knees that interfere with your functioning in everyday life. You may be eager to give up an addiction to cocaine or a habit of constantly interrupting the conversation of other people. But the very first habit you must give up is the habit of self-improvement. You can worry about the other things later. There may be a time and place in your life for self-improvement, but the zendo is not the place, and now is not the time. Put it off.

Giving up self-improvement is easier said than done. Each of us must walk this path alone, going nowhere. But as your teacher, I can suggest to you some skillful means by which you may at last break the habit of mending your ways, and I can offer you some guidelines by which you may measure your

APPENDIX

progress on this pathless path.

I would like to ask that you take two weeks of your life to devote yourself to relinquishing self-betterment. If you conscientiously follow the eightfold path which I here describe, I am confident you will be pleased with the lack of results.

1. As soon as you get up in the morning, stand before the mirror, look your reflection in the eye, and ask yourself ten times, "Who wants to be a better person anyway?"

2. Before going to sleep each night, tell yourself ten times, "Every day in every way I am getting less attached to self-improvement."

3. For these two weeks, withdraw from all therapy programs, yoga classes, harpsichord lessons, courses in wilderness survival, or other educational pursuits. There will be time to pick up where you left off, when you are free from the need to achieve.

4. For the duration of the program, do not follow any special diets. Make a half-hearted attempt to eat whatever is lying around the house forgotten. This is the time to use up the jar of cocktail onions, the stale crackers, the rest of those little silver balls for decorating cakes, and other such things you may find in the back of the cupboard.

5. Walk slowly in place for twenty minutes a day, while repeating monotonously, "There is no attainment, with nothing

to attain." It takes a full twenty minutes for your body to register the fact that it is not benefiting either from an increased heart rate or the secretion of stress-reducing epinephrines into the bloodstream. This is an advanced practice, demanding constant mindfulness so that you don't go anywhere or get any exercise. At first you may need to check your pulse periodically to be sure that it stays the same.

6. Keep a chart on which you daily mark as high or low your level of attachment in the following areas:

> mentally healthy interpersonal interactions
> physical well-being
> productive work
> spiritual enlightenment

Remember, you are looking for *low attachment,* not *high achievement.*

7. From the daily TV program guide, select the program that interests you the least. Be honest with yourself. Then watch this program with a glazed expression. More advanced students should tape the program on a VCR and watch it a second time.

8. Sit on a round black cushion and face the wall. Don't think about anything. Breathe.

If you will follow these instructions with meticulous effort,

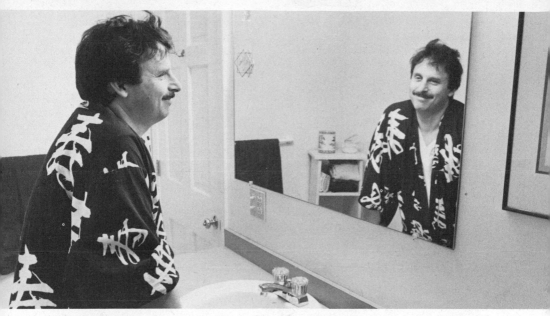

As soon as you get up in the morning, stand before the mirror, look your reflection in the eye, and ask yourself 10 times, "Who wants to be a better person?"

Before going to sleep each night, tell yourself ten times, "Every day in every way I am getting less attached to self-improvement."

you will find at the end of two weeks that you have not only failed to improve, but you have given up the very idea of self-improvement, perceiving it at last for the hopeless task it really is.

I respectfully ask you not to waste your time. You may delude yourself by promising to give up self-improvement soon, *after* you have stopped biting your fingernails, lost ten pounds, or learned to jitterbug. This is a trap. Tomorrow it may be too late—in the final stages of the disease, the sufferer loses all control and those around him find themselves hiding course catalogues and health-club brochures. Bush Wak told the young monk to take a nap *immediately*. Remember, you are perfect already, exactly as you are. In a manner of speaking. And if you were really perfect, you wouldn't have a friend in the world.

GLOSSARY

Asana   A contorted physical posture assumed by a yogic practitioner.

Ashram   A hindu commune.

Birkenstocks   A kind of ridged sandal, imported from Germany, and formerly much in fashion among new age types.

Bodhidharma   An ancient and fierce Buddhist patriarch who brought Buddhism from India to China. He achieved notoriety by cutting off his eyelids in order to keep from falling asleep while sitting zazen.

Bodhisattva   A compassionate being who works for the enlightenment of all, and who is easily taken advantage of.

Buddha nature   Suchness.

Chakra   According to ancient yogic wisdom, there are seven chakras, or energy nodes, in the human body, starting at the base of the spine and going up to the top of the head. The chakras have been officially recognized by Western medicine ever since 1971, when a team of surgeons attempting a hair transplant on Swami Mahaha discovered a tiny trap door at the top of his scalp. When they opened it, a beam of light shone forth, emitted by a small flashlight.

Dharma   The truth, the teaching. Also, phenomena, stuff, including everything that's in the attic waiting for the next yard sale.

Dokusan   A supposedly private interview between roshi and student.

Gatha   The Buddhist version of the limerick, usually composed for a particular occasion.

Half lotus, full lotus   Cross-legged postures for seated meditation, in which one or both feet, respectively, are raised on the opposite thigh, and humiliation of the flesh is thereby achieved.

Heart Sutra   One of the most essential Buddhist scriptures, chanted at almost every service. This sutra contradicts itself repeatedly and denies the existence of practically everything.

Jukai   A ceremony in which a person officially becomes a Buddhist and receives a Buddhist name and telephone number.

Kalpa   A long period of time, a week longer than an eon.

Karma   The law of cause and effect, often used as an excuse or explanation for something apparently inexplicable, as in, "That's just his karma."

Kensho   The moment the alarm goes off and the sleeper awakes.

Koan   A teaching story or question, often from an old Zen tale, which confounds logic and helps the student to feel desperately confused.

Makyo   A vision occurring in zazen.

Mantra   A short verbal formulation, with power in its repetition, sometimes passed on from guru to student in exchange for money.

Miso   A paste of soybeans that makes an excellent soup, if you like that sort of thing.

Mudra   A hand position with special meaning, not usually referring to obscene gestures.

Net of Indra   A symbol of the connectedness of all things. Each seemingly separate thing is but a knot in the net, a wart on the weft, a bug in a rug, a bump on a log.

Nirvana   It's even better than satori.

Oryoki   Set of three nesting bowls and utensils used for formal meals in the zendo. The word is a contraction of *Oreo cookie*, because in strict traditional practice, the first bowl was used for the top wafer, the second bowl for the bottom wafer, and the third bowl for the cream filling.

Rakusu   A bib for a Buddhist.

Roshi   Zen master; venerable teacher.

Samadhi   A state of deep concentration, achieved primarily through meditation and computer games.

Sangha   The community of practitioners; the home team.

Satori   An enlightened state of consciousness, far far beyond what mere words could ever convey.

Sesshin   An intensive Zen meditation retreat, often compared to the experience of having extensive root-canal work done.

Setsu stick   A small spatulalike utensil used for cleaning one's eating bowls after formal Zen meals. A home away from home for bacteria.

Shikantaza   An aggravating method of zazen in which one tries not to think.

Soji   A flourishing of brooms and dust rags in a Zen center.

Soto Zen   A school of Zen Buddhism founded in Japan in the thirteenth century by Dogen.

Sutra   A Buddhist scripture.

Tatami   A straw mat.

Theravada   The Southern school of Buddhism, prevalent in Southeast Asia.

Tofu   A tasteless food item made from cubic soybeans.

Vipassana   Theravadin meditation practice.

Zabuton   A meditation mat, on top of the tatami, under the zafu.

Zafu   A throw pillow for a zendo.

Zazen   An acronym for *Zero Action for Zealots and Earnest Nerds.*

Zendo   A room in which nothing is ever accomplished.

ABOUT THE AUTHOR

In real life, such as it is, Susan Moon lives with her two sons in Berkeley, California, where she teaches, writes, and tries to see things as they are. She has been a member of the Berkeley Zen Center for many years. As hard as she searched, she never found Tofu Roshi, and so she had to make him up.